HANGED $_{AT}$
BIRMINGHAM

STEVE FIELDING

First published 2009

The History Press
The Mill, Brimscombe Port
Stroud, Gloucestershire, GL5 2QG
www.thehistorypress.co.uk

British Library Cataloguing in Publication Data.
A catalogue record for this book is available from the British Library.

ISBN 978 0 7524 5260 9

Typesetting and origination by The History Press
Printed in Great Britain

CONTENTS

ABOUT THE AUTHOR

Steve Fielding was born in Bolton, Lancashire in the 1960s. He attended Bolton County Grammar School and served an apprenticeship as an engineer before embarking on a career as a professional musician. After many years of recording and touring, both in Great Britain and Europe, most notably with punk rock band The Stiffs, he began writing in 1993 and had his first book published a year later. He is the author of eighteen books on the subject of true crime, and in particular hangmen and executions.

He compiled the first complete study of modern-day executions, *The Hangman's Record 1868–1964* (Chancery House Press, 1994) and, as well as writing a number of regional murder casebooks, he is also the author of two books on executioners: *Pierrepoint: A Family of Executioners* (Blake 2006) and *The Executioner's Bible: Hangmen of the 20th Century* (Blake 2007). He has worked as a regular contributor to magazines such as the *Criminologist*, *Master Detective* and *True Crime* and as the Historical Consultant on the Discovery Channel series *The Executioners*, and *Executioner: Pierrepoint* for the Crime & Investigation channel. He has also appeared on *Dead Strange* (Southern Television) and BBC1's *The One Show*. Besides writing he also teaches at a local college.

Hanged at Birmingham is the sixth in a series and follows *Hanged at Durham*, *Hanged at Pentonville*, *Hanged at Liverpool*, *Hanged at Manchester* and *Hanged at Leeds*. Forthcoming titles include: *Hanged at Wandsworth* and *Hanged at Winchester*.

Previous titles in the series:

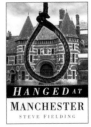

ACKNOWLEDGEMENTS

I would like to thank the following people for help with this book. Firstly Lisa Moore for her help in every stage in the production, but mainly with the photographs and proof-reading. I offer my sincere thanks again to both Tim Leech and Matthew Spicer, who have been willing to share information along with rare documents, photographs and illustrations from their own collections. Thanks also to Stewart McLaughlin for help with information on the prison. I would also like to acknowledge the help given by Janet Buckingham, who inputted some of the original data, and Gillian Papaioannou, who proof-read and helped edit the final draft.

I would like to thank Ted Rudge and Mac Joseph, both of whom run excellent websites dealing with the history of Birmingham. I would also like to thank Mary Woodroffe for helping with information on numerous cases, and to the many people who contacted me offering information on cases featured in this book.

RESEARCH MATERIAL & SOURCES

As with my other true crime books, many people have supplied information and photographs over the years, a number of whom have since passed away. In particular, I remain indebted to the help with rare photographs and material by assistant executioner Syd Dernley and prison officer Frank McKue.

The bulk of the research for this book was done many years ago with information added to my database as and when it has become available. In most instances contemporary local and national newspapers have supplied the basic information, supplemented by material found in PCOM, HO and ASSI files held at the National Record Office at Kew and the Home Office Capital Case File 1901–1948, along with personal information in the author's collection gathered from a number of those directly involved in some of the cases.

Space doesn't permit a full bibliography of books and websites accessed whilst researching *Hanged at Birmingham*. I have tried to locate the copyright owners of all images used in this book, but a number of them were untraceable. In particular, I have been unable to locate the copyright holders of a number of images, in the main those sourced from the National Archives. I apologise if I have inadvertently infringed any existing copyright.

INTRODUCTION

HMP Birmingham, formerly known as Winson Green Gaol, is one of the largest gaols in the country. Serving Magistrate and Crown Courts in Birmingham, Stafford and Wolverhampton along with the magistrates' courts of Burton, Cannock, Lichfield, Rugeley, Sutton Coldfield and Tamworth, it currently holds around 1,000 male prisoners. Its notable inmates have included rock star Ozzy Osbourne and multiple murderer Fred West, who hanged himself in a cell here on New Year's Day 1995.

During the Victorian era, as the Industrial Revolution spread throughout the Midlands, and its population grew rapidly, more and more criminals were tried in the town of Birmingham and, following conviction, transported to Warwick to serve their sentence or face execution. It was a costly measure and in 1845, Birmingham council decided it was time to build a new gaol to replace the inadequate one currently in use.

Birmingham's first gaol had been situated on Peck Lane, on what is now the site of New Street railway station. When that closed in 1806, prisoners were transferred to a new prison attached to the public offices in Moor Street, on what is now the site of Moor Street station. When this gaol became too small to cope with the demands imposed on it, councillors searched for a new site, finally settling on a seven-acre piece of land on Winson Green Road, in the ward of Soho.

Designed by architect Daniel R. Hill, the new gaol was built in the 'panoptican' design with wings radiating away from a central tower. This modern design, pioneered by Russian factory bosses overseeing production lines, allowed a warder standing in the central area a clear view down each wing from that one central position. Featuring a gothic-style gatehouse that gave the building the appearance of a medieval castle, it became known as the Borough Gaol, and work was finally completed in 1849.

The first governor at Winson Green was Edinburgh-born Captain Alexander Maconochie, a former naval officer and pioneer in penal reform. Maconochie had been taken prisoner during the Napoleonic Wars before becoming a professor of geography at the University of London in 1833. Whilst serving on convict ships and ashore in Van Diemen's Land, Maconochie had formulated and then operated the mark system, which became the cornerstone of modern English prison discipline. In 1847, having previously published a number of books on prison reform, Maconochie was allowed to carry out his proposal for the use of convict labour to construct a harbour at Weymouth.

Maconochie was unjustly dismissed in 1851, following a visit from government officials, from reports made into the treatment of prisoners at the gaol. He was replaced by his

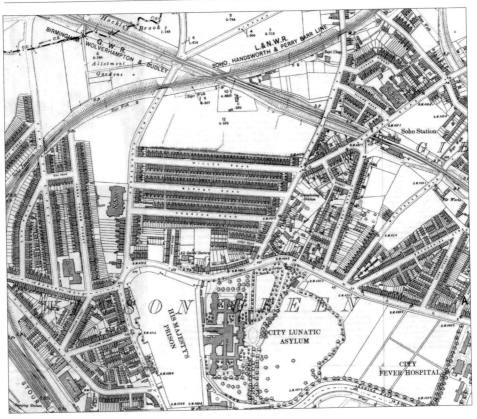

An Ordnance Survey map of Winson Green in the late Victorian era. (Crime Picture Archive)

second in command, Lieutenant Austin RN, but conditions at the gaol were soon in the news again, when a Royal Commission was set up following the suicide of three young prisoners at the gaol. The scandal had first broken, and the conduct of discipline at the gaol questioned, following revelations at the inquest of 15-year-old Edward Andrews, who had hanged himself in his cell on 7 April 1854.

At a public meeting, allegations of severity and cruelty were made by two recently dismissed members of the prison staff. The Home Secretary, Lord Palmerson, was petitioned and informed that:

> If a criminal must suffer death it should be by the doom of the law, and the sentence should be carried out in a legal manner, but not form part of any system that a man or any set of men should have the power to inflict such a prison discipline as will daily lessen the prisoner's love of life, until finally goaded to madness, and no longer able to endure that discipline, he consummates his life of crime by the great crime itself of self-destruction.

Although the proceedings of the Royal Commission focused primarily on the activities of Governor Austin, the commissioners questioned both present and previous staff, along with former and present prisoners of the gaol. Their findings uncovered a legacy of severity and illegal punishment, leading back to the regime of Captain Maconochie,

Captain Maconochie, the first governor
of Birmingham Borough Gaol.
(Crime Picture Archive)

although the report ended with both Governor Austin and the prison surgeon being heavily censured and facing charges for their actions at the gaol. Both were removed from post and the prison settled back into a more or less normal routine.

In July 1913, the prison was again in the news when Prime Minister Herbert Asquith came to the area to address a gathering at Staffordshire's Bingley Hall. Suffragette groups, incensed at his lack of activity in the field of Women's Suffrage, stormed the venue, smashing windows at the hall as he spoke, and as a result six women were arrested and imprisoned at Winson Green, where, as was often the norm, they went on hunger strike.

*

Birmingham became an assize town in 1884, five years before Queen Victoria elevated it to a city, and holding an assizes meant it would also need to employ an executioner to deal with convicted murderers. Like other gaols around the country, Birmingham did not retain its own executioner. Instead, the under-sheriff of the local county in which the condemned prisoner had been sentenced to death, retained a copy of the short Home Office list of hangmen and assistants and selected an executioner from that, with the prison governor being responsible for recruiting the assistant executioner. Initially the hangman worked alone, but by the turn of the century it became the norm to employ an assistant at all executions.

MEMORANDUM OF INSTRUCTIONS FOR CARRYING OUT AN EXECUTION

1.   The trap doors shall be stained a dark colour and their outer edges shall be defined by a white line three inches broad painted round the edge of the pit outside the traps.

2.   (a) A week before an execution the apparatus for the execution shall be tested in the following manner under the supervision of the Works Officer, the Governor being present:-

    The working of the scaffold will first be tested without any weight.   Then a bag of dry sand of the same weight as the culprit will be attached to the rope and so adjusted as to allow the bag a drop equal to, or rather more than, that which the culprit should receive, so that the rope may be stretched with a force of not more than 1,000 foot-pounds.   See Table of Drops.   The working of the apparatus under these conditions will then be tested.   The bag must be of the approved pattern, with a thick and well-padded neck, so as to prevent any injury to the rope and leather.   Towelling will be supplied for padding the neck of the bag under the noose.   As the gutta percha round the noose end of the execution ropes hardens in cold weather, care should be taken to have it warmed and manipulated immediately before the bag is tested.

    (b) On the day before the execution the apparatus shall be tested again as above, the Governor, the Works Officer and the executioner being present.   For the purpose of this test a note of the height and weight of the culprit should be obtained from the Medical Officer and handed to the executioner.

3.   After the completion of each test the scaffold and all the appliances will be locked up, and the key kept by the Governor or other responsible officer; but the bag of sand should remain suspended all the night preceding the execution so as to take the stretch out of the rope.

4.   The executioner and any persons appointed to assist in the operation should make themselves thoroughly acquainted with the working of the apparatus.

5.   In order to prevent accidents during the preliminary tests and procedure the lever will be fixed by a safety-pin, and the Works or other Prison Officer charged with the care of the apparatus prior to the execution will be responsible for seeing that the pin is properly in position both before and after the tests. The responsibility for withdrawing the pin at the execution will rest on the executioner.

6.   Death by hanging ought to result from dislocation of the neck.   The length of the drop will be determined in accordance with the attached Table of Drops.

7.   The required length of drop is regulated as follows:-

    (a) At the end of the rope which forms the noose the executioner should see that 13 inches from the centre of the ring are marked off by twine wrapped round the covering; this is to be a fixed quantity, which, with the stretching of this portion of the rope, and the lengthening of the neck and body of the culprit, will represent the average depth of the head and circumference of the neck after constriction.

    (b) While the bag of sand is still suspended, the executioner will measure off from the painted lines on the rope the required length of drop and will make a chalk mark on the rope at the end of this length.   A piece of copper wire fastened to the chain will now be stretched down the rope till it reaches the chalk mark, and will be cut off there so that the cut end of the copper wire shall terminate at the upper end of the measured length of drop.   The bag of sand will then be raised from the pit, and disconnected from the rope.

(The chain ......

Memorandum for carrying out an execution. (Author's collection)

The chain will now be so adjusted at the bracket that the lower end of the copper wire shall reach to the same level from the floor of the scaffold as the height of the prisoner. The known height of the prisoner can be readily measured on the scaffold by a graduated rule of six foot six inches long. When the chain has been raised to the proper height the cotter must be securely fixed through the bracket and chain. The executioner will now make a chalk mark on the floor of the scaffold, in a plumb line with the chain, where the prisoner should stand.

(c) These details will be attended to as soon as possible after 6 a.m. on the day of the execution so as to allow the rope time to regain a portion of its elasticity before the execution, and, if possible, the gutta percha on the rope should again be warmed.

8.   The copper wire will now be detached, and after allowing sufficient amount of rope for the easy adjustment of the noose, the slack of the rope should be fastened to the chain above the level of the head of the culprit with a pack-thread. The pack-thread should be just strong enough to support the rope without breaking.

9.   When all the preparations are completed the scaffold will remain in the charge of a responsible officer until the time fixed for the execution.

10.   At the time fixed for the execution, the executioner will go to the pinioning room, which should be as close as practicable to the scaffold, and there apply the apparatus. When the culprit is pinioned and his neck is bared he will be at once conducted to the scaffold.

11.   On reaching the scaffold the procedure will be as follows:-

   (a)   The executioner will:-

      (i)   Place the culprit exactly under the part of the beam to which the rope is attached.

      (ii)   Put the white linen cap on the culprit.

      (iii)   Put on the rope round the neck quite tightly (with the cap between the rope and the neck), the metal eye being directed forwards, and placed in front of the angle of the lower jaw, so that with the constriction of the neck it may come underneath the chin. The noose should be kept tight by means of a stiff leather washer, or an india rubber washer, or a wedge.

   (b)   While the executioner is carrying out the procedure in paragraph (a) the assistant executioner will:-

      (i)   Strap the culprit's legs tightly.

      (ii)   Step back beyond the white safety line so as to be well clear of the trap doors.

      (iii)   Give an agreed visual signal to the executioner to show that he is clear.

   (c)   On receipt of the signal from his assistant the executioner will:-

      (i)   Withdraw the safety pin.

      (ii)   Pull the lever which lets down the trap doors.

12.   The body will *THEN* be carefully raised from the pit ~~as soon as~~ *PROVIDED* the Medical Officer declares life to be extinct. Then the body will be detached from the rope and removed to the place set aside for the Coroner's inspection, a careful record having first been made and given to the Medical Officer of both the initial and final drops. The rope will be removed from the neck, and also the straps from the body. In laying out the body for the inquest the head will be raised three inches by placing a small piece of wood under it.

WILL HANG FOR A MINIMUM OF 45 MINUTES, AND

Memorandum for carrying out an execution (continued from previous page). (Author's collection)

There were numerous applicants for the position of hangman once it became known that a gallows would be installed at Winson Green, but the position had never been vacant. The first hangman to officiate at the gaol was former Bradford policeman James Berry. Berry had been the country's chief executioner since 1884 and, a few weeks prior to his first visit to Birmingham, he had been involved in one of the most sensational executions in the annals of capital punishment when the gallows failed to open during an execution at Exeter. Three times the condemned man, John 'Babbacombe' Lee, was lead to the gallows and each time the drop failed to open. An enquiry later found that the gallows had been hastily constructed using thinner wood than normal and, situated in the open air of the prison yard, heavy rain had swollen the wooden trapdoors on the gallows so that when the weight of the prisoner was placed on the traps they swelled slightly and were locked tight.

The first execution shed at Birmingham was a brick-built building standing in the prison grounds. Resembling a detached garage, it was erected in front of the southern wing of the gaol, some forty yards from the condemned cell. A local newspaper wrote that the platform was constructed on ground level inside the small, whitewashed brick apartment, with the trapdoors occupying almost all the floor area. The doors were 6ft wide and 9ft long, divided into two horizontal flaps. Beneath the doors were three strong metal hinges held in place by metal staples. When the hangman pulled the lever the hinges would slide and the bars would reach a recess in the support bar and allow the doors to fall. Across the platform, at a height of about 8ft, stood a crossbeam built into the walls and onto which the executioner secures the ⅝in-thick, hempen rope. Access to the pit below was via a small trapdoor, which opened on to steps leading below.

The original execution shed situated in the grounds of Birmingham Gaol would have been similar to this one at London's Newgate Prison. (Prison Service Museum)

EXECUTIONS —TABLE OF DROPS (October, 1913).

The length of the drop may usually be calculated by dividing 1,000 foot-pounds by the weight of the culprit and his clothing in pounds, which will give the length of the drop in feet, but no drop should exceed 8 feet 6 inches. Thus a person weighing 150 pounds in his clothing will require a drop of 1,000 divided by 150=6⅔ feet, i.e., 6 feet 8 inches. The following table is calculated on this basis up to the weight of 200 pounds :—

TABLE OF DROPS.

Weight of the Prisoner in his Clothes.	Length of the Drop.		Weight of the Prisoner in his Clothes.	Length of the Drop.		Weight of the Prisoner in his Clothes.	Length of the Drop.	
lbs.	ft.	ins.	lbs.	ft.	ins.	lbs.	ft.	ins.
118 and under	8	6	138 and under	7	3	167 and under	6	0
119 ,,	8	5	140 ,,	7	2	169 ,,	5	11
120 ,,	8	4	141 ,,	7	1	171 ,,	5	10
121 ,,	8	3	143 ,,	7	0	174 ,,	5	9
122 ,,	8	2	145 ,,	6	11	176 ,,	5	8
124 ,,	8	1	146 ,,	6	10	179 ,,	5	7
125 ,,	8	0	148 ,,	6	9	182 ,,	5	6
126 ,,	7	11	150 ,,	6	8	185 ,,	5	5
128 ,,	7	10	152 ,,	6	7	188 ,,	5	4
129 ,,	7	9	154 ,,	6	6	190 ,,	5	3
130 ,,	7	8	156 ,,	6	5	194 ,,	5	2
132 ,,	7	7	158 ,,	6	4	197 ,,	5	1
133 ,,	7	6	160 ,,	6	3	200 ,,	5	0
135 ,,	7	5	162 ,,	6	2			
136 ,,	7	4	164 ,,	6	1			

When for any special reason, such as a diseased condition of the neck of the culprit, the Governor and Medical Officer think that there should be a departure from this table, they may inform the executioner, and advise him as to the length of the drop which should be given in that particular case.

All hangmen were issued with a table of drops, but an experienced executioner would use his own skill and judgement rather than rely on these. (Author's collection)

James Berry's first job at Birmingham was the hanging of Henry Kimberley, at which the local press dubbed Berry unpleasantly talkative and boastful. A few weeks after he had hanged Kimberley, Berry was back in the region for the execution of Moses Shrimpton, an elderly poacher sentenced to hang at Worcester Gaol. Berry badly botched the execution and the old man's head was torn from his body when the drop fell. It was one of several unpleasant experiences Berry had as an executioner and when a similar incident happened at Liverpool in 1891 he tendered his resignation.

James Billington succeeded Berry as the country's chief executioner and made several visits to Birmingham in the latter years of the reign of Queen Victoria. Early in the twentieth century James's son, William, carried out two executions at the gaol, assisted on the first by his younger brother, John. In 1913, after almost a decade since the last execution at the gaol, Tom Pierrepoint made his first trip to Birmingham, for the execution of Frank Greening. Pierrepoint would make a total of ten visits to the gaol and, in 1936 he hanged the only woman to be executed at Birmingham, poisoner Dorothea Waddingham, who went to the gallows for the murder of two elderly ladies in her care.

Although Henry Pierrepoint, the country's chief executioner for most of the first decade of the twentieth century, never officiated at Birmingham, two other hangmen did pull the lever at Birmingham around this time. John Ellis, who had assisted William Billington in 1904, carried out half a dozen executions during and shortly after the time of the First World War, including, on one occasion, an execution without an assistant. In 1926, William Willis made two appearances at the gaol. A veteran of over twenty years service as a hangman, Willis's career was now coming to an end and he was noted by one prison governor to be bloody-thirsty and callous, having taken to drinking heavily, which had caused his once toned physique to become bloated. At the execution of John Fisher, Willis claimed he had been so eager to get the execution over with that he almost secured the noose around a prison guard – causing one of the most sensational blunders in modern execution history. Willis was dismissed for misconduct later that summer.

Probably the most famous of modern day executioners, Albert Pierrepoint, made his professional debut as an assistant at Birmingham, at the execution of Jeremiah Hanbury in 1933. Despite what Pierrepoint may have claimed, when he penned his biography in the 1970s, his role on this occasion was purely as a non-participating observer. He assisted his uncle several times at the gaol before carrying out a number himself as chief executioner in the post-war years. Pierrepoint resigned in 1956 and was succeeded by Harry Allen, who carried out the remaining executions at the gaol following the Homicide Act of 1957; although the previous two executions, both during the time Albert Pierrepoint was still active as an executioner, were offered to and accepted by Steve Wade. It was at the execution of Ernest Harding in 1955 that the governor noted Wade's eyesight was failing and a few weeks later, when this information reached the prison commissioners, Wade was dismissed on medical grounds 'as a precaution against what may happen due to his failing eyesight, not because of it.'

A number of local men worked as *both* assistants with one, and Alfred 'Fred' Allen, of Wolverhampton, subsequently became a chief executioner. Allen was a former Coldstream Guard and at his first official execution as an assistant, at Swansea in December 1928, he had fallen through the trapdoors when he failed to step back far enough once he had strapped the prisoner's legs. (It was because of this incident that Albert Pierrepoint, one of the next batch of assistants to join the list, was made to attend an execution as an observer, to familiarise themselves with procedures before being deemed competent enough to carry out the job.) Allen had assisted just a handful of times before he was entrusted with the responsibility of chief executioner at Oxford in 1932. He carried out just three jobs before he died in around 1937. In his later years he had been working as a caretaker at Wolverhampton labour exchange while working as a hangman.

Allen had graduated from the executioner's training school at London's Pentonville Prison in 1928, along with another local man, Frank Rowe of Birmingham. Rowe had applied for the post in February 1928, and at the time of application he was 45 years old and had served for twenty-five years in the Coldstream Guards: seeing action both in South Africa and in the First World War, during which time he had been a prisoner of war. In a long, distinguished military career, he had been awarded numerous bravery

LIST OF CANDIDATES REPORTED TO BE COMPETENT FOR THE OFFICE OF
EXECUTIONER, OR WHO HAVE ACTED AS ASSISTANTS AT EXECUTIONS.

Name and Address.	Remarks.
Thomas W. Pierrepoint, Town End, Clayton, Near Bradford, YORKSHIRE.	Has satisfactorily conducted execut[...], has assisted at executions, and [...] been practically trained at Pentonville Prison.
Robert Baxter, 10, Balfour Street, Hertford.	Has satisfactorily conducted executions; has assisted at executions, and has been practically trained at Pentonville Prison.
Robert Wilson, 15, Barnard Road, Gorton Mount Estate, Manchester.	Has assisted at executions, and has been practically trained at Pentonville Prison.
Thomas M. Phillips, 203, Albert Road, Farnworth, Bolton, Lancs.	Has assisted at executions, and has been practically trained at Pentonville Prison.
Henry Pollard, 15, Longfield Street, Blackburn. LANCS.	Has assisted at executions, and has been practically trained at Pentonville Prison.
Lionel S. Mann, 91, Milkstone Road, Rochdale, LANCS.	Has assisted at executions, and has been practically trained at Pentonville Prison.
Frank Rowe, M.M. 1/241, King Edwards Road, Ladywood, Birmingham.	Has been practically trained at Pentonville Prison.
Alfred Allen, 2, Park Street South, Blakenhall, Wolverhampton.	Has been practically trained at Pentonville Prison.

This list of executioners dating from 1929 shows two local men, Frank Rowe and Alfred Allen, as qualified assistants. (Author's collection)

and good conduct medals including the Military Medal. Although at his interview he was noted as being sullen and not endowed with any fine feeling, he nevertheless successfully overcame the medical and passed the training.

Rowe's name was to stay on that short list of executioners for just a matter of weeks. In January 1929 he was engaged as assistant to Tom Pierrepoint at Durham. Quite what Rowe had expected or had been told during his training is unclear, but he was shocked to find that he was expected to remain in the prison on the night prior to the execution and to pay for his own transport to the gaol, and to claim it back on arrival. He penned a scathing letter to the prison commissioners, blaming them for incompetence and for expecting him to pay his own fare and not making clear his duties. A report from the governor at Durham came back that Rowe had arrived at the prison at 8.25 p.m. on the night prior to the execution, not before 4 p.m. as he had been instructed to do so. He also noted that Rowe was slow and hesitant at the execution, but put that down to his inexperience. The report said that Rowe had had ample time to make enquiries as to what was expected of him once he received the engagement. Whatever response the commissioners made to his letter, Rowe never officiated at another execution.

The next local man to join the list was Herbert 'Harry' Allen, an ice-cream seller from Selly Oak, who had made numerous applications to join the list before finally being accepted for training in 1948. Following training, he and the other successful candidates, Sydney Dernley and George Dickinson, attended as observers at the execution of James Farrell in 1949.

Allen was to have just a brief stint as an assistant and in 1951 he apparently told the prison commissioners that his boss at the ice-cream works had told him to choose between that job or working as an executioner. Allen chose to remain in his day-to-day job, but was alleged to have later begged Pierrepoint to help get his name added back to the list. It wasn't.

Harry Robinson of Kingswinford became an assistant in 1956, and carried out his observation at Birmingham a year later, when he watched Dennis Howard go to the gallows. Robinson assisted at one of the last executions in August 1964, at Liverpool, and continued to be offered work as an assistant up until abolition in 1965. He also made a number of television appearances, always incognito, claiming that even his closest family were unaware of his role as an executioner.

*

Although the original scaffold had been erected in the grounds of the gaol, by the 1930s the gallows, in line with the rest of the country, had been moved indoors and was now situated on C wing, with the condemned cell and gallows on landing 2, and the pit below on landing 1. It was at Birmingham that a tale originated that has since passed into prison folklore. One prisoner, about to be lead outside to the original gallows, supposedly said as he reached the door leading to the courtyard, and observing the heavy rain, 'Well, I don't fancy going out in that!' A warder beside him then replied, 'I don't know what you are complaining about, I've got to walk back in it!'

For a city the size of Birmingham, the number of executions that took place here is relatively small, compared to gaols like Manchester, Leeds and Liverpool for example. This was mainly on account of the region having a number other provincial gaols that continued to execute prisoners well into the twentieth century. Warwick, Worcester,

The interior of a modern execution chamber. The sandbag is filled to the weight of a prisoner. It is left suspended overnight to remove any stretch from the rope. Beyond the drop the folding wooden doors, painted yellow, would be removed on the morning of the execution, exposing a corridor that lead to the condemned cell. It would be a walk of just a few paces from cell to gallows. (Author's collection)

Stafford, Nottingham and Leicester all played host to the hangman and resulted in the gallows at Winson Green being less active than would otherwise have been the case.

*

In recent times, the prison has come under much criticism for its conditions, with the Chief Inspector of Prisons for England and Wales describing conditions at Winson Green as some of the worst ever seen. It was said in a recent report by the Chief Inspector to be the second most overcrowded prison in England and Wales, operating over its maximum capacity of just under a 1,000 inmates. Newspapers reported it had one of the worst regimes in England and Wales, with prisoners let out of their cells on 'association' for just five hours a week.

A BBC report later claimed ministers had ignored appeals to improve the Victorian prison and conditions had deteriorated since the last highly critical report. In what appeared to be harking back to the troubles of a century before, a large proportion of inmates – approximately 11 per cent – claimed to have been assaulted by officers, with one mentally ill prisoner repeatedly denied a shower or change of clothing as staff believed he was faking illness.

Many of those hanged at Winson Green heard sentence of death passed on them at Birmingham Assize Court. (Crime Picture Archive)

The prison has recently undergone a period of considerable change as a result of a multi-million pound investment programme by the Prison Service. The prison population has almost doubled and new workshops, educational facilities, a healthcare centre and gymnasium have been added in attempts to improve existing facilities. The Grade II listed gatehouse was also replaced and removed to storage.

This book looks in detail at the stories behind the forty men and one woman who were all *Hanged at Birmingham*.

Steve Fielding, 2009
www.stevefielding.com

1

MURDER ON PARADISE STREET

Henry Kimberley, 17 March 1885

By the December of 1884 relations between 53-year-old Henry Kimberley and 39-year-old Harriet Stewart had all but broken down. They had been together for seventeen years, meeting shortly after Kimberley had parted from his wife. Kimberley had a skilled job as screw toolmaker at Periam & Co. on Floodgate Street and the income he earned allowed them to take a house at 24 Pershore Road, Birmingham. Although they were able to enjoy a comfortable lifestyle, their days became more and more fraught with quarrels and tantrums and as Christmas approached, it was decided they would part.

They consulted solicitors and a bond was drawn up which allowed Harriet Stewart, who sometimes used the name Stevens, to retain possession of the house, while Kimberley would keep a piano and receive £20. He also agreed not to interfere with her in any way and on 18 December he packed the remainder of his belongings and left Pershore Road.

Almost at once Kimberley began to rue the decision and tried to get the agreement cancelled, but it was in vain. He made repeated pleas with Harriet to reconsider but the short time they had been apart had been the first days she had spent without fear of getting into an argument or facing his wrath, and she told Kimberley she preferred her new life.

Kimberley took this rejection badly and began to drink heavily. He was heard making threats that if she wouldn't take him back he would kill her. A few days before Christmas, he was drinking in the Gem Vaults on Steelhouse Lane when Harriet Stewart entered. They shared a drink and he was later overheard by the barmaid threatening to kill Harriet if she maintained her refusal to take him back. It seems Harriet didn't take these threats seriously and went about her life seemingly without fear for her safety.

Late on the night of Boxing Day, Harriet was asleep beside her daughter when Kimberley forced an entry into the house. Harriet woke to find him standing at the bottom of bed. He pleaded that he was cold, hungry and had spent the money granted in their separation order. Kimberley remained in the house until the following morning, when Harriet's sister came over and told him to leave. Harriet and her sister had an appointment that afternoon at Riley's Musical Instrument Warehouse on Constitution Hill with regard to the piano referred to in their agreement, and when Kimberley learned about this he travelled to the shop and was there waiting when the women arrived. Outside the shop he again pleaded with Harriet to take him back. Finally her patience snapped.

Henry Kimberley, the first man to be hanged at Birmingham.
(T.J. Leech Archive)

She told him she had no intention of changing her mind and that he must accept her decision.

That evening Harriet met up with an old friend, Emma Palmer, in the Gem Vaults, one of a number of public houses run by Emma's husband, Thomas. A short time later, at around 7 p.m., Harriet, Emma and Emma's two daughters left the Vaults and travelled to another of Thomas Palmer's pubs, the White Hart on Paradise Street.

Kimberley had somehow discovered where they were drinking and soon followed. He immediately begged Harriet to come home, but she again bluntly refused. He then turned to Emma Palmer and asked her to persuade Harriet to come back with him, but she refused to get involved. Over the next hour, Kimberley made a number of attempts to get Harriet to change her mind, each request being met by the same firm refusal.

Finally, Kimberley made to leave but then paused and turned, calmly addressing Harriet: 'Have you determined whether you are going to live with me again or not?'

She simply shook her head and replied, 'No, I am not!'

At that Kimberley pulled a gun out of his pocket and pointed it at Harriet. He fired once; the bullet struck her a glancing blow to the head, sending her crashing to the ground. Harriet tried to stand, but collapsed in a heap. Emma Palmer jumped from her seat and went to her friend's aid and as she stood over the stricken Harriet, Kimberley pointed the gun again and fired. Emma was struck in the neck. She screamed and staggered down the bar trying to stifle the blood gushing from the vicious wound.

Pot-man Harry Parsons, serving in the bar, witnessed the shootings and, with little thought for his own safety, dashed towards the gunman and tried to detain him. Kimberley wasn't going to be held without a struggle and began to fight with Parsons, the fight spilling into the main bar, where another customer came to the barman's assistance. Despite now being outnumbered, Kimberley fought hard against the younger men until an off-duty policeman was alerted to the disturbance and, after placing Kimberley under arrest, took him into custody.

Both women were taken to the Queen's Hospital, where Harriet soon made a recovery. Emma clung on to life for two weeks until she suffered a relapse. Doctors told Thomas Palmer his wife's condition was serious and he hurried to her bedside, arriving moments before she passed away. Kimberley had been held in custody charged with attempted murder and this was then amended to a charge of wilful murder.

At Kimberley's trial before Mr Justice Field at Birmingham Assizes at the end of February 1885, the defence tried to suggest that the gun had gone off accidentally, but it was a hopeless case as the prosecution called witnesses who had heard the threats he had made prior to the shooting and others who had been present on the night of the shooting. Proceedings were short and the jury needed only a few moments to debate their verdict and find the prisoner guilty as charged. There was no recommendation of mercy.

Following conviction, Kimberley was taken to Winson Green Prison and housed in the condemned cell. He would be the first man to be hanged in the town for almost eighty years. The last execution in Birmingham had been in August 1806, when Philip Matsell had been hanged at Snow Hill for the attempted murder of a 'night-watchman', a forerunner to the modern policeman. A crowd of over 40,000 had gathered to watch that execution.

As the day of Kimberley's execution approached, several letters were received applying for the post of executioner. One man, a local Sunday school teacher, even sent his certificates as proof of his steadiness and trustworthiness, but there was no vacancy and hangman James Berry of Bradford had already been engaged to carry out the sentence.

Kimberley was resigned to his fate and while awaiting the hangman he actually put on over a stone and a half in weight. Despite popular belief that prisoners lost weight (through stress), this was quite common: many prisoners lose weight under the fear of the forthcoming murder trial and it is only once the verdict has been decided and the path to the gallows looms closer that the prisoner seems to regain an appetite.

At the appointed hour, once Berry had secured his wrists, Kimberley walked firmly to the scaffold and, as he took his place on the trapdoors, he began praying ardently.

'Lord receive my soul, Lord be merciful,' Kimberley begged as the hangman pushed the lever sending the prisoner to his doom. Berry had allowed a drop of 8ft 3ins and death was reported to be instantaneous due to severance of the spinal chord. A crowd, which witnesses claimed varied in numbers between 5,000 and 15,000, congregated outside the

Hangman James Berry.
(Author's collection)

prison gates and stood in silence until the black flag was hoisted to show that the Paradise Street murderer had paid the full penalty of the law.

2

THAT FATAL NIGHT

George Nathaniel Daniels, 28 August 1888

'I intended to shoot her. I love the ground she walks on and if she gets over this I will marry her!'

Statement by George Daniels following his arrest for attempted murder.

In the winter of 1887, George Daniels took lodgings in Castle Street, Birmingham. Twenty-nine-year-old Daniels, a widower who worked as a printer's porter at Britten's stationers on High Street, soon made the acquaintance of Emma Hastings, the 21-year-old daughter of William Hastings, a Birmingham publican who ran the Golden Elephant public house close to Daniel's lodgings on Castle Street. Daniels and Emma began courting and when Daniels left Castle Street to lodge with a workmate on Conybere Street, he continued to make daily visits to the pub to sit with Emma when she helped out behind the bar or played the piano for the benefit of the customers in the smoking room.

It seemed to everyone the Daniels and Emma would marry; her parents liked him and he was given free run of the house and would often stay behind after closing time, helping to clear the glasses. As Daniels began to spend more time in the bar so he began to drink more and more and on one occasion Emma chastised him in front of a number of regulars, telling him, 'If you drink so much whisky it will drive you mad. You are not the same when you have had that wretched stuff.'

On Saturday evening, 14 April 1888, Daniels called at the Golden Elephant and at 9.30 p.m. he was seen chatting pleasantly enough with Emma in the sitting room at the back of the pub. They were then joined by Emma's younger sisters, Alice and Louisa, and at closing time Emma sat in the kitchen plaiting Alice's hair. Daniels had his coat on and was preparing to leave. He asked Emma to see him to the door and she told him to wait until she had finished plaiting the hair. He then walked over to her, kissed her on the cheek, stepped back a couple of paces, pulled out a gun and fired two shots.

One bullet struck Emma in the chest, the other smashed into her skull. Alice's screams brought neighbours rushing into the kitchen and Daniels was soon overpowered. As Emma was taken to the General Hospital he was taken into custody where he was charged with attempted murder. In his pocket were a razor, a handful of bullets, a number of letters and photographs of Emma.

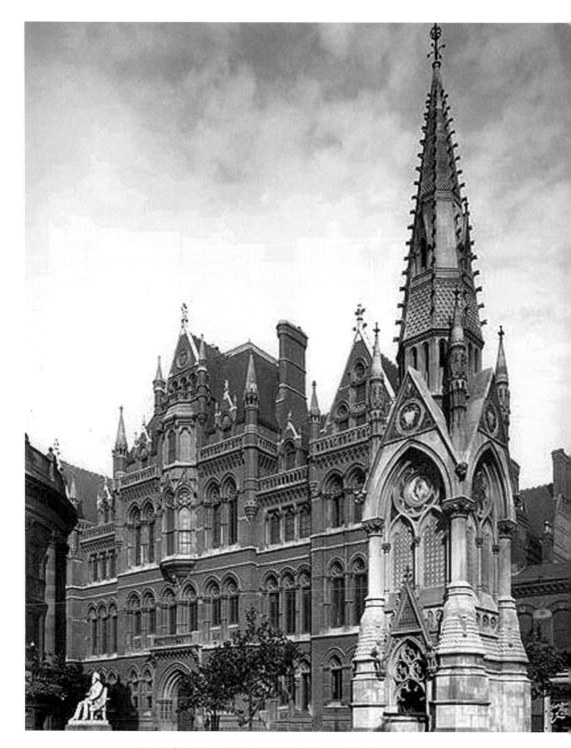

Birmingham General Hospital. (Crime Picture Archive)

The following morning he confessed that he shot her and gave a motive for the attack: 'I have been trying to break it off. I couldn't carry on any longer, it cost me a lot of money going to the house and treating the people there.' He then added that he hoped she recovered and that he still wanted to marry her.

On the following day Daniels was brought up before the stipendiary magistrate at Birmingham Police Court. He seemed so overcome by what had happened he could barely walk and had to be half carried into the dock, where, with his head bowed and in floods of tears, he listened as the court was told that Emma Hastings had been shot by the prisoner and was not expected to live.

On Thursday 19 April, Emma regained consciousness and when interviewed by detectives she declined to make either a formal statement or a deposition, saying she didn't want to get Daniels into trouble. She was still very weak and doctors cut short the interview, as the bullet was still lodged in her head and they were unable to remove it. On the following afternoon Emma's condition suddenly worsened and with her family at her bedside she died from her injuries. Daniels broke down in tears when he heard the news and he was now informed he would be charged with murder.

At his trial, before Mr Justice Wills on Saturday 4 August, a defence of insanity was offered. His counsel told the court that Daniels had been widowed several years before and been left with two young children. His wife's death had affected him badly and he had tried to commit suicide on a number of occasions. They said there was no motive for the crime and that Daniels had been drinking and was unaware of his actions.

The prosecution claimed there was indeed a motive and referred to the statement Daniels had made following his arrest in which he confessed to shooting her and that he wanted to end their relationship. They also called witnesses who claimed that Emma had frequently quarrelled with Daniels on account of his drinking and gambling.

Following the judge's summing up it took the jury just ten minutes to reach their verdict. Daniels was found guilty of wilful murder, and asked if he had anything to say before sentence was passed, he nodded and said, 'It was not wilful murder, my Lord, nor do I remember one bit on that fatal night.'

3

THE LODGER

Henry Benjamin Jones, 28 August 1888

When George Richard Harris became friends with Harry Jones, he could never have imagined the terrible events that would happen just a few years later that would lead to Jones dying at the end of the hangman's rope.

The two had met in the spring of 1884 while working for contractors Messrs Lucas and Aird erecting gas tanks in Windsor Street, Birmingham. Harris was 29 years old at the time, Jones eight years younger, and, when he learned that his friend was about to be made homeless, Harris offered Jones lodgings at the home he shared with his wife and three children on Park Lane, Aston. It seems there was an instant attraction between Jones and Harris's wife, Sarah Annie, and in due course the two soon embarked on a clandestine affair.

While Jones soon found himself out of work, Harris was busy working as a carpenter and, with his skills much in demand, he was often asked to work away. Returning from one trip, Harris discovered his wife's unfaithfulness and, while he attempted to come to terms with things, he sent her and the children to stay with his parents in Gloucester. Unbeknown to Harris, Jones followed Sarah and the children and they soon rekindled their romance.

When Harris finished his latest contract he travelled to Gloucester where he was enraged to find Jones had recently visited. They had a fierce quarrel and came to blows and ultimately Sarah Harris, after then having a fierce quarrel with Jones, in which he shot and wonded her, returned to Birmingham alone. Jones was sentenced to three months' imprisonment for the affray.

In April 1887, while her husband was working away in Monmouthshire, Sarah took possession of 29 Meriden Place, off Sutherland Street, in the shadows of Aston railway station and overlooking the main London & North West railway line. Jones, who had since been released from prison and made his peace with Sarah, helped her move the furniture in and neighbours were told that he was her half-brother.

It seems that George and Sarah must have continued together as a married couple despite living apart and his working at various times in Nottingham and South Wales, for when Sarah found herself pregnant Harris believed that the child, christened Florence Mabel, was his own. Jones also believed the child was his. In the spring of 1888, Sarah also gave birth to a son, christened William, and again it seems that both Harris and Jones believed the child was theirs.

In June 1888, after several months of unemployment, Jones found work at Oldbury Carriage Works, but any happiness he may have felt at finally getting back on his feet was soon dashed on Monday 11 June, when he was given a note at work from Sarah telling him to stay away from Meriden Place as her husband had arrived home unannounced. Jones took lodgings at a friend's house on Sutherland Road and, on Tuesday, he went to the carriage works and asked to be paid up. As he had only worked a few days he was told to come back on the following day.

Having collected what he was owed on Wednesday, Jones called into W.B. Anning's bicycle shop on Steelhouse Lane and purchased a six-chamber revolver and twenty cartridges for 5s, telling salesman William Anning that he wanted the weapon to scare the cats away from his rabbits and also as a precaution against thieves. Returning to his temporary lodgings, he spent the night drinking and writing a letter in which he claimed he had been deceived by a married woman who had told him she would never go back to her husband.

On the Thursday morning, Jones went round to Meriden Place and threw stones at the window and, when Harris came outside, Jones pulled out his gun and fired. As Harris

THE TERRIBLE SHOOTING CASE AT ASTON N^R BIRMINGHAM—FOUR PERSONS INJURED

WHERE HARRIS WAS SHOT | PRISONER | THE HOUSE IN MERIDEN PLACE | FIRING HIS LAST SHOT | LITTLE GIRL VIC

HARRIS FLYING FROM JONES | JONES MURDEROUSLY ATTACKS M^{RS} HARRIS | ATTACKING THE INFANT

How the Illustrated Police News *covered the case of Harry Jones. (Author's Collection)*

rushed back inside the house Sarah came out and Jones pointed the gun at her and fired once, striking her in the shoulder. Jones then climbed through the downstairs window and further shots rang out. When Sarah staggered inside, she found her young daughter, Florrie, lying on the floor bleeding from a horrific head wound. The young boy, William, had also been shot and beaten with what appeared to be the butt of the gun. All four were taken to hospital and, although Harris and Sarah, along with baby William, recovered from their wounds, Florrie remained in a serious condition for ten days before she succumbed to her injuries on 25 June.

The case was subject to some debate before Jones came to trial, when it was announced in the newspapers that councillors in Birmingham didn't want to burden the taxpayers of the town with the cost of the trial and wanted a county jury at Warwick to preside over the proceedings. It was eventually decided to hold the trial in the town and Jones pleaded insanity when he appeared before Mr Justice Wills at Birmingham Assizes on Monday 6 August. He was charged with the wilful murder of Florence Harris and the felonious shooting, with intent to kill, of George, Sarah and William Harris. It was a straightforward case for the prosecution; witnesses had seen Jones with the gun after hearing sounds of shots and Jones had admitted to the arresting officer that he had carried out the shootings.

Sarah Harris told the court that two days before the shootings Jones had spoken to her and made the chilling boast: 'I shot you once, and I will do so again. I am going to swing for you!' The jury needed just twenty minutes to deliver their verdict. Jones turned pale when sentence of death was pronounced over him and he had to be escorted from the dock.

Jones was hanged alongside another killer who had used a firearm, George Daniels (*see* Chapter 2). They were housed in adjacent cells, but did not meet each other until a few hours before execution, when they breakfasted together before walking bravely to the gallows. Once the drop fell, Daniels died instantly, but in the case of Harry Jones it was several minutes before doctors certified death. One witness later claimed that he had struggled for over four minutes on the drop, his death agonies terrible to witness.

4

'WHAT WOMEN DRIVES YOU TO'

Frederick Davis, 26 August 1890

The condemned man was giving his guards and prison officials a great deal of concern. Since his conviction for murder, 37-year-old Fred Davis had spent the days awaiting his execution in a terrible state. He was unable to eat and could barely sleep for more than a few minutes before he would wake in tears, sweating and trembling both with fear and from the effects of his abrupt withdrawal from alcohol.

Davis had had an unhappy marriage, due in most part to his intemperate habits, and as a result, in the spring of 1890, 34-year-old Mary Ann Davis had left her husband several times and on each occasion had gone to stay with her sister on Ashton Road, Birmingham. So bad had her husband's drinking become that for the last three weeks he had been in almost a continual drunken stupor.

Fred Davis was gunsmith who lived with his wife and five children at 3 St Stephen's Place, St Stephen's Street, off Newton Row, Birmingham. The couple had been married for eighteen years. Davis had held a steady job at Richard Readman's on Vauxhall Street and in previous years he had earned as much as £8 per week, a very good sum in those days, but since the end of 1888 he had turned to drink and had changed from a loving family man into, as it was stated in the papers, 'a beastly drunk'.

On Friday morning, 16 May 1890, Davis left home and made his way to work, where at lunchtime his 13-year-old son, Freddy, arrived with his dinner. Davis told his son he was going to see his aunt, Davis's sister, Sarah Ward, who lived with her husband John in a courtyard off Aston Road.

When Freddy returned home later that afternoon he told his mother what Davis had said, and, believing he would be trying to borrow money to buy drink, Mary put on her hat and coat and made her way to her sister-in-law's. Arriving at the house she found her husband was already there, carrying a Martini-Zeller rifle (sometimes known as a rook and rabbit rifle), which was wrapped in a blanket. She told him to come home and in the company of Sarah Ward, the couple made their way back to St Stephen's Street.

Wary that his brother-in-law was carrying a rifle, John Ward decided to follow them and when he reached the house, they were already sat in the parlour, with Davis sending Freddy out to get more beer, having put the rifle in the other room.

Mary then turned on her husband and pleaded with him to curb his drink and to take care at work as she was afraid that his frequent absences due to drink would lead to him being dismissed. Davis listened for a few moments before getting to his feet and storming out. The others continued to chat and gave little thought about Davis until John Ward heard what sounded like a trigger being pulled.

Davis then re-entered the room carrying the rifle. Mary had been stooping down beside the door and, upon seeing the gun in his hand, she exclaimed, 'Oh, Fred, what on earth are you going to do with that gun?' She had barely finished speaking when Davis squeezed the trigger and a bullet hit Mary in the mouth, sending her crashing back to the floor. He reached into his pocket and pulled out a bullet, and made to reload, but Ward jumped to his feet and wrestled with the gunman, managing to disarm him.

A neighbour, hearing the sound of a shot, saw Mary staggering to her feet with blood oozing from her mouth, and turned on her heels in search of a policeman. As Mary stumbled out into the yard before succumbing to her injuries, Davis walked into the courtyard and shouted, 'I have done it at last, goodbye.'

A police constable arrived within minutes and called out, 'Where is the man?'

'It's me. I'm here,' Davis said calmly as he leaned against a wall. 'It was me that did it. I'm not going to run away. You see what women drives you to.'

Davis was placed under arrest and taken to Duke Street police station, where it was reported that he kept raising his handcuffed hands to his head as if trying to remember something, and stared wild-eyed at the officers questioning him.

Davis appeared before the fearsome Mr Justice Hawkins at Birmingham Assizes on Wednesday 6 August. The court heard that Davis had a recent history of abusing his wife since becoming addicted to drink. On one occasion she had been admitted to hospital following a head wound; another time he had brought home a sword and threatened to 'run her through' with it, and shortly before he shot her, Davis had thrown a paraffin lamp at her.

The jury took just fifteen minutes to return their guilty verdict and, as he passed sentence of death, the judge told the prisoner there was no hope of the sentence not being carried and to expect no mercy.

The fearsome Mr Justice Hawkins sporting the black cap he wore when sentencing prisoners to death. (Author's collection)

Davis's death certificate, showing cause of death due to judicial execution. (Mary Woodroffe)

Davis seemed to take these words to heart and made for a distraught and terrified prisoner. It was believed amongst the prison officers that he wouldn't live long enough to face the hangman, but Davis did finally rally. He began to eat his meals, his weight increased and he spent his final days much more composed, taking great comfort from the words of the chaplain.

5

THE BRIDE-TO-BE

Frederick William Fenton, 4 April 1894

Florence Nightingale Elborough was looking forward to her forthcoming marriage. The 29-year-old barmaid and her fiancé, 32-year-old Fred Fenton, had already secured a home, at 50 St James Street, in the Lozells district of Birmingham and, on Saturday 9 December 1893, accompanied by her brother, she and Fenton had gone to the Old Church at Smethwick and paid 3s to have the bans published. With the wedding set for Wednesday 3 January 1894, they began to make preparations to furnish the house before the big day.

Smethwick Old Church, where Fred Fenton and Florence Elborough were due to wed. (Crime Picture Archive)

Although Fenton earned a decent living as a silversmith, he appeared to have exaggerated his financial status somewhat to his bride-to-be and, seemingly believing him to be more prosperous that he actually was, she began compiling a list of large items she would like for the house.

On the following Monday, Fenton left his home on Buckingham Street and called into a pawnbrokers where, for 4*s* 6*d*, he purchased a six-chambered revolver and fifty cartridges. That afternoon he went to see Florence, who lived-in and worked at the Plough and Harrow Inn on Hampton Street. Anyone who knew the couple thought them perfectly matched; no one had seen them arguing, or heard a cross word between them in public, and today was no different. They spent some time together talking before Fenton left. On the following morning, Fenton called at the Plough and Harrow and told Florence that he was unwell, suffering from neuralgia and toothache. She told him he would be too late to start his shift if he didn't hurry and he said that if his head was better, he would go in at 9 a.m. Fenton left soon after but did not go to work. Instead, with his brother-in-law, he went to St James' Street, where they measured up blinds and floor coverings. As Fenton was taking off his coat, his brother-in-law noticed the handle of a gun protruding from his jacket pocket and asked, 'Why, Fred, what's the meaning of this?'

'I'm not going to harm anybody,' Fenton replied, adding, 'I'm going to settle a dog that's bit me!'

At 6.15 p.m. Fenton was back at the Plough and Harrow where the landlord's wife, Winifred Sanson, saw him sitting with Florence in the back parlour. They appeared to be on good terms and a short time later Florence went up to her room to put on her hat and coat, telling Winifred that she was going out for a walk. No sooner had she returned downstairs than shots rang out from the parlour. Winifred hurried downstairs and found both Florence and Fenton lying on the floor. Florence had been shot several times in the head. One bullet had split her lip and knocked several teeth out; another had embedded itself in her head, entering above the ear, while a third had struck her in the breast.

Fenton had then turned the revolver on himself and shot himself through the mouth, with the bullet exiting through the jaw, knocking off his hat and embedding itself in the ceiling.

Both were hurried to the local hospital and neither was at first expected to survive. Gradually both improved and on 23 December, Florence was visited by detectives, but declined to make a statement. On the following day she succumbed to her injuries. Detectives also interviewed Fenton and when they informed him that Florence had died, he simply replied, 'I can't account for how I did it.'

Fenton was discharged from hospital on 2 February and removed to Winson Green, where he was held pending his court appearance, which was scheduled to take place before Mr Justice Baron Pollock on Saturday 17 March at Birmingham Assizes.

The prosecution offered a motive for the crime, saying that Fenton had promised to buy certain items for the house and as a result Florence had ordered them and needed the money to settle the invoices. On the day of the murder, he had promised her he would bring the £10 she needed to pay the creditors, but had turned up without the money. It was alleged that she had then challenged him as to why he was so reluctant to spend any money. Unable to admit that he was not as solvent as his fiancée believed, possibly due to his being on short time at work, he had decided upon drastic measures. He had then shot Florence, mortally wounding her, before turning the gun on himself.

His defence was that he was suffering from a nervous disorder and that his mind was unhinged. The jury needed just thirty minutes to return their verdict.

'With regret we find the prisoner guilty,' the foreman told the court.

While Fenton was awaiting execution petitions were made to the Home Secretary asking for him to be spared, and the Home Office directed two medical experts to visit the prisoner to assess his mental condition. They found that he was sufficiently sane and there were no grounds for recommending a reprieve due to insanity.

Fenton bore up well and walked bravely to the gallows on a cold and dismal April morning. Hangman James Billington arrived at the prison having conducted two executions on the previous days: on Easter Monday he had executed a woman at Liverpool who had murdered her husband, and on the following day had hanged an ex-soldier at Leeds. Fenton was given a drop of 7ft 3ins and death was reported to be instantaneous. The body was left to hang for one hour and a second measurement was taken before the body was removed from the rope and made ready for burial. This found an increase of 16in, made up of the 'stretch' in the rope (usually an inch or two with a new rope) – the remainder being from the prisoner's neck!

Mr Justice Baron Pollock, who passed sentence of death on Fred Fenton. (Author's collection)

Hangman James Billington made his first visit to Winson Green in 1894. (Author's collection)

The LPC4 sheet detailing Fenton's execution shows that after hanging for one hour there was an increase in sixteen inches from the length of the original drop. Much of this would be the stretch caused by breaking the prisoner's neck. (Author's collection)

6

A TERRIBLE THING

Frank Taylor, 18 August 1896

On the evening of Tuesday 10 March 1896, 10-year-old May Lewis failed to return to her home on Smith Street, Birmingham, after leaving school. Her father searched the streets in vain before calling the police.

At 6 a.m. the following morning, John Williams was making his way to work. His route took him along Hyde Street, in what was known as the jewellery quarter of the city and, as he passed the front door of the house at 93 Vyse Street, he saw what appeared to be a young girl, covered in blood and sitting in the garden close to the doorway. As he approached he could see that her clothes were torn and blood was still oozing from a number of wounds to her face and arms.

The police were notified and officers were quickly at the scene. A police surgeon, Dr Burton, certified that the young girl was dead and a post-mortem found that her skull was fractured and she had been brutally raped.

Blood trails from where the body was found led to the door of 93 Vyse Street, and officers banged on the door, alerting the elderly occupants, caretaker John Taylor and his wife. Entering the hallway they found more traces of blood and a thorough search of the house suggested that the child had been attacked in an upstairs bedroom. It seemed some attempt had been made to clear up the bloodstains and in the old couple's bedroom a bloodstained rag was found hidden in the water tank.

Detectives arrested Mr and Mrs Taylor, who protested their innocence. As they were being taken to the police station they told officers about their 23-year-old son, Frank, who had visited the house yesterday begging for money to pay his rent. They told officers that their son was a loafing, good-for-nothing fellow, who had lodgings in the city.

A search was made for Taylor, who was described as 5ft 7ins tall, wearing a blue serge jacket, brown corduroy trousers and a black billycock hat. The hunt was barely a few hours old when Taylor walked into Dudley Road police station and confessed to the murder of the young girl. His clothing was soaking wet and it soon became clear he had tried to drown himself in a canal only for passers-by to pull him to safety. Taylor claimed that reports in that day's newspaper, which covered the murder, were inaccurate and when asked to clarify he simply said, 'I shall not say anything now; I will say it later.' He then made a simple statement which was to show the callous nature he maintained throughout his imprisonment, trial and execution: 'What a fuss about a bloody kid!'

When Taylor appeared at Birmingham Assizes before Mr Justice Wills on Thursday 30 July, the prosecution based their case purely on circumstantial evidence. They claimed that Taylor had lured the young girl into the empty house and tried to rape her. When she resisted, he had beaten her death with a brick before dumping her body outside. He then made a failed attempt to take his own life, before confessing to police as a search for the murderer was underway.

A witness had identified Taylor as the man seen in the company of a young girl entering 93 Vyse Street at 5.30 p.m. on the day that May Lewis had disappeared. Taylor's parents told officers that their son had been drinking when he called at their house, and the court heard how John Taylor, the prisoner's father, had told them, 'this is a terrible thing for me. I know I have done wrong, I ought to have informed the police ...'

The jury took just a few minutes to reach a verdict and Taylor stood seemingly unconcerned as sentence of death was passed upon him. He maintained this callousness throughout his last days awaiting execution, sleeping soundly at night and eating his meals with relish.

A large crowd gathered outside the prison gates on the morning of the execution, including the victim's mother, dressed in full mourning clothes. As the fateful hour of 8 a.m. neared, shouts and jeers broke out cursing Taylor and his dreadful crime. On the stroke of eight, as the black flag unfurled at the top of the flagpole, a loud cheer rang out with many of the crowd clapping in appreciation of the hangman's work.

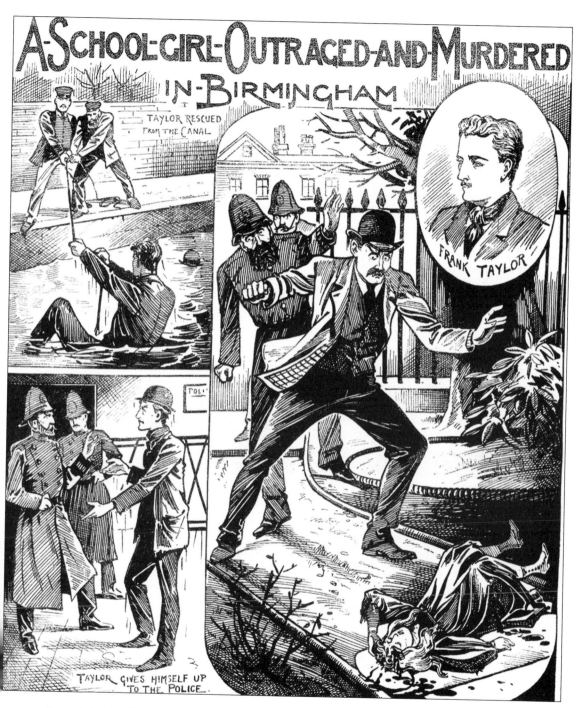

Frank Taylor's horrific child murder made the front page of the Illustrated Police News. *(Author's collection)*

SECRET EXECUTION AT BIRMINGHAM.

A JURYMAN'S STATEMENT.

Frank Taylor, a labourer, aged 23, was executed at Birmingham on Tuesday morning for the murder of a little girl ten years old, named May Lewis, on March 10th. The child did not return home from school, and the next day her mangled body was found in an area in front of a house occupied by the prisoner's parents. Upon the house being searched by the police the bed and floor were found to be covered with blood. Evidence showed that the prisoner decoyed the child into his parents' house on the evening of March 10. Efforts were made to obtain a reprieve, but the Home Secretary declined to interfere with the sentence. Prior to his conviction the culprit gave a considerable amount of trouble to the prison officials, frequently bounding from his bed in the night in a frantic manner. After his conviction, however, he became more calm, and at times showed traces of penitence. On Saturday, when he had his final interview with his parents, he was much shaken, although he did not absolutely give way. Billington was the executioner, and there were present at the fulfilment of the sentence only the under-sheriff and the chief gaol officials, the Press being again excluded. The

FRANK TAYLOR.

Above: *Frank Taylor was the first of many child-killers to meet their death on the gallows at Winson Green. (Author's collection)*

Left: *A news cutting detailing the execution of Taylor, at which the press were not invited. (Author's collection)*

The LPC4 sheet shows that Billington botched Taylor's execution and that the cause of death was due to asphyxia and not by dislocation of the spine. (Author's collection)

7

THE FEUD

John Joyce, 20 August 1901

The feud had been long standing. For over two years, the bad blood had simmered until, in the summer of 1901, it led to an assault and criminal proceedings. Thirty-six-year-old labourer and former soldier John Joyce had been involved in a dispute with his neighbour, 61-year-old John Nugent and his sons, who lived in a courtyard on Price Street, Birmingham. On Friday 7 June 1901, Joyce found himself in court charged with assault on one of the Nugents and now, even though he had been discharged, he wanted revenge. In the early hours of the following Monday, Joyce turned up at the Nugents' house staggering around in a drunken state. The Nugents' next-door neighbour, Emma Moore, knew John Joyce well. She was aware of the quarrels between Joyce and the Nugents, so when she saw Joyce approach the old man's house she confronted him and asked him what he was up to. Joyce mumbled that he must have gone to the wrong house and turned away.

At 8 p.m. that evening, Joyce returned to Price Street and began making threats to the old man, who was in the house alone. Mrs Moore saw him hammering on the Nugents' front door and saw it opened. John Nugent begged Joyce to go away, but the ex-soldier was drunk and hell-bent on trouble. Picking up a paraffin lamp, he threw it at Nugent. As the lamp exploded into a ball of flames, the old man rushed out into the street, pursued by Joyce, who pulled out a carving knife and stabbed him in the chest, shouting, 'Take that!' Nugent staggered back several paces and slumped to the ground. He died on his way to the infirmary, by which time Joyce had been taken into custody.

Joyce's trial at Birmingham before Mr Justice Phillimore on 31 July was little more than a formality. Neighbours on Price Street had positively identified him as the assailant and the court heard about the long-standing feud between Joyce and the Nugent family, which had resulted in court proceedings just three days before the murder.

Joyce pleaded insanity as a result of the sunstroke he had suffered whilst serving in India. It was to no avail and there was only one possible verdict, although the jury did add a recommendation of mercy, believing that Joyce had been provoked by the Nugent family and that had ultimately led to the murder. Nevertheless, at Winson Green Gaol on a warm summer morning, as a crowd of almost 3,000 congregated outside the prison gates, Joyce walked to the gallows and the feud was finally ended.

8

THROUGH JEALOUSY

Charles Samuel Dyer, 5 April 1904

It was on Boxing Day 1903 that Charles Hammond, a 25-year-old ex-soldier turned hawker, met 21-year-old Martha Eliza Simpson. Preferring to use the name 'Pattie', Wolverhampton-born Martha worked as a prostitute, and although Charles was aware of how she earned her living, the couple soon moved in together, taking a room in Hurst Street, Birmingham, in a lodging house run by the mother of Martha's close friend, Maggie Moran. Early in the New Year they found a place of their own, close by, when they rented a small cottage at 2 Back 21 Inge Street, Birmingham.

Hammond's real name was Dyer and it was under this name that he had been discharged 'with ignominy' from the army at Birmingham on 19 December 1903, after serving over eight years; three with the Royal Artillery including lengthy service in Malta, before ending his service in India with the 1st Warwickshire Regiment.

Charles Dyer. (Author's collection)

On the afternoon of Wednesday 3 February 1904, Martha and Maggie had lunch with Dyer at their home and later that day Dyer went out to a pub, returning in the early evening with a number of items he asked Martha to pawn for him. Martha and Maggie called at the pawnbrokers and obtained a shilling, which they handed over to Dyer.

Dyer then went to Cuttler's beerhouse on the corner of Station Street, in the company of Arthur Lockley, who lodged at Mrs Moran's on Hurst Street. With Dyer out drinking, Martha decided to procure a little business and soon found a client, whom she took back to Maggie's home at 15 Birmingham Place, off Bristol Street.

Shortly after 11 p.m., Dyer and Lockley made their way to Birmingham Place, passing on the street as they approached the front door Martha's young client. Dyer by this time was unsteady on his feet, and no sooner had he arrived at the house than he got into a row with Martha about her continuing to work as a prostitute, shouting, 'I give you five shillings a day to keep you, not for you to go out whoring.' They then went outside, where she managed to pacify him, and around midnight they left the house hand-in-hand.

Fifteen minutes later Dyer was back at the house where he announced, 'Oh Maggie, I've done it. Save her if you can.' Maggie, and several others present at the house, hurried to Dyer's home on Inge Street, where they found Martha slumped in an armchair with a horrific throat wound. Once Dyer was in custody he confessed that he was very much in love with the woman, and had became angry when he learned that she had been in the company of another man that evening.

When the trial took place at Birmingham on 17 March before Mr Justice Wills, Dyer's defence claimed that he was so sodden with drink he had been unaware of what he was doing. His counsel claimed there was no premeditation, but the prosecution put forward a case of a man driven to commit murder through jealousy, when the woman he loved continued to work as a prostitute. There was no recommendation to mercy and William

William Billington (left) and his brother John (right) both followed in their father's footsteps to become Chief Exceutioners in the early twentieth century. (Author's collection)

Billington, assisted by his brother John, hanged Dyer on a warm spring morning as a large crowd congregated outside the main gate. In line with recent government rulings, there was no tolling of the bell or raising of the black flag, and the only intimation that the execution had taken place was when the notices were posted on the prison gates to state that Dyer had been executed according to law.

9

IN THE HEAT OF THE MOMENT

Samuel Holden, 16 August 1904

Samuel Holden had served his country well during the Boer War and had ended his service with a distinguished record, being awarded the South African Medal with four clasps. He had also been wounded in action. Returning to England, he found work as a market porter and lived in a variety of dwelling houses with his girlfriend and part-time prostitute, Susan Humphries. By the summer of 1904, they were in rooms at 2 Back 109 Coventry Street, in a run-down part of Birmingham.

Both 32-year-old Holden and Humphries, two years older, were alcoholics and, following bouts of heavy drinking, they would frequently quarrel. These rows were so commonplace, and increasingly more violent, that neighbours began to speculate that something serious would happen. Happen it did, on Saturday 2 July, when a neighbour living across from the couple's rooms, Eliza Walton, heard sounds of a struggle in the passageway. She opened her door and saw Holden pull out a knife and stab Susan several times in the chest before dropping the knife and running out into the street, shouting, 'Fetch a doctor. I've killed her!' A doctor was duly summoned, followed closely by police officers, but despite medical assistance Susan Humphries died on the way to hospital.

Holden's defence, when he appeared before Lord Chief Justice Alverstone at Birmingham Assizes on 29 July, was one of provocation. He maintained that he had stabbed Susan in the heat of the moment, following a quarrel when she had failed to provide him with an adequate meal when he returned home from work. The evidence against him was never really questioned, but in his summing up, the judge sympathetically referred to Holden's war record, remarking that whilst his previous life had entitled him to every consideration, the case must be tried on its merits alone. The jury were told to consider only the evidence they had heard in court, not what may have happened before. After twenty minutes deliberation, the jury returned and announced that Holden was guilty of murder.

The former soldier maintained his courage on the morning of his execution, puffing on an expensive cigar as he walked firmly to his death.

10

'BIRMINGHAM LIZZIE'

Frank Greening, 13 August 1913

On 20 March 1913, 27-year-old Elizabeth 'Lizzie' Hearne attended a party at the home of her close friend, Edith Mumford, at 21 Ashley Street, Birmingham. A short time later, Frank Greening, a 34-year-old painter, and Lizzie's sometime boyfriend, turned up and Edith's mother invited him inside, showing him to the sitting room where Elizabeth and Edith were chatting. A few minutes later, Edith excused herself and left the room, leaving Greening and Lizzie alone. She returned a few minutes later to find Greening hurrying out of the house. Edith dashed into the sitting room and found her friend lying on the floor, her clothing set alight by a smashed paraffin lamp. Edith quickly extinguished the flames but Elizabeth required medical treatment and needed bandages to cover her wounds.

One lunchtime, two weeks later, Edith Mumford and her stepfather, Frederick West, called into the Queen's Head pub where Lizzie Hearne and Annie West, Edith's mother, later joined them. Greening was also there and later left with Edith's stepfather, telling them he was going home. West soon returned to the pub holding a postcard on which Greening had scribbled a message in pencil containing threats against Lizzie.

After reading the card, Lizzie and Edith finished their drinks and headed for Edith's house at 5 Back 115 Bissell Street. They met up with Ida Bolding, a tenant at the house, and all three were sitting chatting when Greening burst in carrying a gun. They began to quarrel over a house key and Lizzie, angry at the threats he had made against her, shouted that she was 'not frightened of that shooter either.'

Greening, who had put the gun in his jacket pocket while he was talking, suddenly withdrew it and fired three shots at Lizzie. He then pointed the gun at Edith and fired one more shot.

The bullets hit Lizzie in the thigh, stomach and shoulder; Edith had been lucky, in her case the shot missed and smashed into the wall. Lizzie was rushed to hospital where Greening, disguising himself as a relative, visited her and tried to persuade her not to press charges. He fled when the alarm was raised and made his way to a friend's house, where he confessed what he had done.

The police launched a hunt for Greening and later that night, Detective Constable Henry Jones spotted the wanted man in Claybrook Street and placed him under arrest. Greening had by now disposed of the gun and denied firing the shots when he was taken into custody and charged with attempted murder. This changed to a full murder charge when Lizzie died from her wounds on the following day.

Greening stood trial for murder at Birmingham Assizes on 14 July, before Mr Justice Atkin. The court heard that Greening had met Lizzie, who was commonly known as 'Birmingham Lizzie', while they were both in London. He moved to Birmingham and wrote to her inviting her to join him in the Midlands and she accepted the offer. They lived in a number of slums around the city and frequently argued. On several occasions he was heard making threats to kill her.

The prosecution built their case mainly on the testimony of eyewitnesses and the statement Greening had made following his arrest when he told officers; 'We had a few words and on impulse I pulled out the gun and shot her.' Following conviction the court heard that in 1894 Greening had served five years for the wounding of

BIRMINGHAM MURDERER HANGED.

EXECUTION AT WINSON GREEN.

LAST CHAPTER IN A SQUALID STORY.

The first execution for nine years took place at Winson Green Prison yesterday morning, when Frank Greening, a Birmingham painter, suffered the death penalty for the murder of Elizabeth Ellen Hearne, with whom he had lived. It is now many years since an execution was carried out in public, but at eight o'clock yesterday morning, the time fixed for the execution, there was such a crowd outside the prison as seemed to suggest an expectancy that the spectacle would be a public one. Round the great entrance gates a crowd of many hundreds gathered, and though it became much reduced after the usual official announcement had been made that the law had taken its extreme course, there were still large numbers of people before the prison when the coroner met his jury for the usual inquest.

A news cutting relating to the murder of 'Birmingham Lizzie'. (Author's collection)

Greening was hanged by Tom Pierrepoint, making his first visit to Birmingham. (T.J. Leech Archive)

a woman he had shot with his gun, and in 1901 he had almost killed another woman after hitting her with a jemmy. He was out on licence from prison when he had finally become a murderer.

11

'BETTER TO PART SOONER THAN LATER'

William Allen Butler, 16 August 1916

'Dear Mother. We like one another but it is better to part sooner than later as I am sick of my life.'

Note left by Billy Butler to his mother, May 1916

Florence and George Butler had been separated for over five years when she began a relationship with William 'Billy' Butler. Although not related, Billy and Florence Butler had been acquainted for three or four years, but their friendship developed following her separation, when 29-year-old Florence took her 9-year-old daughter, Nellie, and returned to live with her mother at 2 Bath Terrace, off Chequers Walk, Birmingham.

Ten years older than Florence, 39-year-old Butler was too old to be conscripted and worked as a brass caster at a local munitions works. He had been lodging with Florence's mother, Frances Griffiths, at Bath Terrace since the spring of 1915. Soon after Florence returned to her mother's, in February 1916, they started courting and within weeks Florence found herself pregnant. Her mother had thus far had no problems with Butler while he had been a tenant at the house and raised no objections when told of Florence's condition.

Things soon changed. The couple began to quarrel regularly and the arguments seemed to stem from Butler's being jealous of her. On Saturday afternoon, 20 May, Florence told her mother that Butler had beaten her on the previous day. When Florence showed her mother the bruises on her legs and body, Frances stormed into Butler's room and told him he had one week to find new lodgings or he would be out on the street.

At 6.40 p.m. that evening, Florence had dressed up and was preparing to go out. Butler demanded to know where she was going and with whom. Florence told Butler it was none of his business and headed for the door. Butler returned to his room and, ten minutes later, he also left the house. Florence returned at 9.30 p.m. and was having supper with her daughter and neighbour, Elizabeth Rice, when Butler returned half an hour or so later.

Ten minutes later, Elizabeth bade them goodnight and left the house while Frances went upstairs to get ready for bed. She had been upstairs barely a minute when she heard Nellie begin to scream. As Frances hurried downstairs, Nellie told her that Butler had pulled out a penknife, walked over to her mother and stabbed Florence once in the chest, before calmly walking out.

The police and a doctor were quickly summoned, but Florence Butler was pronounced dead at the scene. A post-mortem conducted later that night found that the cause of death was a single stab wound to the heart. The post-mortem also confirmed that she had been three months pregnant.

Butler was soon in custody. Within the hour he had walked into Ladywood police station and had given himself up as the man wanted for the murder of Florence Butler. Questioned why he had committed the crime, he claimed it was through jealousy of her friendship with an older man named Ireland. Butler said that he suspected she had been to see him that night and when he had returned to the house at 10 p.m. she was eating a crab for supper, which she said Ireland had given her.

At Butler's trial before Mr Justice Avory at Birmingham Assizes on 12 July, the prosecution based their case on the confession he had made following his surrender at Ladywood police station and on the letter found on him addressed to his mother, in which he claimed he was sick of life. This letter was claimed to be tantamount to a confession of murder. At Ladywood, Butler had been shown the penknife and was alleged to have said, 'This is what I did it with and said I would do long ago.'

The bloodstained envelope that contained William 'Billy' Butler's written confession. (TNA: PRO)

*John Ellis hanged Billy Butler on
a sunny August morning in 1916.
(Crime Picture Archive)*

His defence claimed that Butler was driven by jealousy after Florence had confessed of her friendship with Ireland. He had also been in great pain at the time of the murder due to an accident at work and had no recollection of committing the crime.

Found guilty of murder after the jury deliberated for less than an hour, Butler launched an appeal on account of the judge's summing-up, in which it was alleged he had misquoted the confession and this had misguided the jury. The appeal also rejected the claim that, because the victim had confessed to Butler of her relationship with Ireland and that this had driven him to commit the crime, the charge should be reduced to one of manslaughter. Dismissing the appeal, the panel claimed that a reduction to manslaughter on those grounds would only be appropriate if the accused and the victim were man and wife. In this case they were not, as she was still married to a man currently serving his country in France.

A petition to the House of Lords failed, as did a petition of over 7,000 signatures pleading for the Home Secretary to spare his life, and on a warm, sunny August morning, a crowd of over 200 gathered outside the prison gates as Billy Butler was led to the gallows.

12

UNREQUITED LOVE

Louis Van der Kerkhove, 9 April 1918

It was in the spring on 1915 that Belgian couple Pierre Axel and Clemence Verelst fled their homes in Antwerp and sought sanctuary across the Channel. Arriving in Birmingham, both found work in a munitions factory and soon they had put aside enough money to move to London and open a small café. It was here that Clemence made the acquaintance of another Belgian, Louis Van der Kerkhove, also a native of Antwerp. Van der Kerkhove lived in Birmingham, but was in London visiting friends. Clemence and Van der Kerkhove began an affair and he soon persuaded her to leave Axel and join him back in Birmingham, where he had recently taken a position at the Austin works at Longbridge.

She followed him north, but their relationship soon became one of quarrels and fighting, mainly on account of her drinking. On one occasion she even stabbed him in the arm when he told her he was leaving her. Although he neglected to press charges, they parted soon after: she returned to London while he left Longbridge and moved into new lodgings in Dudley.

Within a fortnight Clemence was back in the Midlands and, after tracking Van der Kerkhove down, she managed to persuade him to give their relationship another try. He soon rued the decision: returning home one evening he found she had sold most of his furniture and fled with the money back to London.

Regretting what she had done, Clemence wrote several letters to Van der Kerkhove, apologising for what she had done and declaring her love for him. He refused to be swayed by her pleas for 'one more chance,' but, at Easter 1917, during a trip to London, he did look her up. She asked him to take her back, but he again refused. As they parted, she said she would follow him back to Dudley to get him to change his mind and, a few weeks later, she duly turned up on his doorstep. Over the next few months they continued to live together, but it was not a happy relationship; it seems that they were each jealous of the other. Matters finally came to a head early in 1918.

At 9 p.m. on Sunday evening, 13 January, proprietor Mary Casey was manning the front desk of the Shaftesbury Hotel in Station Street when Van de Kerkhove and Clemence Verelst checked in. She booked them into room ten and an hour later one of the chambermaids heard screams coming from the room. She banged on the door and Van der Kerkhove opened it dressed in just his underwear.

'I have done it now,' he shouted, throwing down a bloodstained dagger. As members of staff went to investigate, Clemence staggered into the corridor crying, 'Help me, I am dying!' She had been stabbed fourteen times.

Belgian murderer Louis Van der Kerkhove. (TNA: PRO)

An ambulance ferried both away from the hotel, stopping at the police station where Van der Kerkhove was taken into custody, while Clemence continued on to hospital. Charged with attempted murder, he claimed that she had driven him to the act by taunting him that she was going to leave him and return to her husband, Pierre Axel, in London. After years of wishing to end the relationship himself, it seemed that finally Van der Kerkhove had fallen in love with the woman. When two days later she succumbed to her injuries, the Belgian was then charged with murder.

At his trial on 18 March at Birmingham, before Mr Justice Lawrence, his defence was one of severe provocation. The court was told that Clemence had treated him badly, stolen money from him and had had affairs with several other men. The prosecution claimed that the murder was simply the result of a jealous quarrel and the prisoner, who had confessed he had killed her in a rage, should face the full consequences of his actions. The jury agreed with the prosecution, and Van der Kerkhove was duly sentenced to death.

13

LIKE JACK THE RIPPER

Henry Thomas Gaskin, 8 August 1919

Even though ninety years have now passed since the horrific murder of a Staffordshire housewife by her husband (which the crime newspapers likened to that of Jack the Ripper), it is still remembered by the people of Hednesford. Long after Henry Gaskin went to the gallows, the woodland where he committed his brutal crime still bears the name Gaskin's Wood, a gruesome reminder of a crime that horrified the whole country when it made the headlines in the spring of 1919.

It was while her husband was away fighting in the First World War that Lizzie Gaskin began an affair with a soldier. By 1918, the 23-year-old mother of three found herself pregnant by her lover and once the child was born she moved from the marital home in Bridgtown, near Cannock, to her mother's house in nearby Hednesford Hill.

Her husband, 25-year-old Henry 'Harry' Gaskin, was finally demobbed following the armistice and in due course returned to Cannock in the winter of 1918. When he discovered his wife's infidelity he decided there was no point returning to Bridgtown so instead he too went back to his mother's home at Hednesford Hill.

On Wednesday 19 February 1919, Gaskin, now working as a miner at West Cannock Colliery, met up with an old friend in a local pub and after a couple of drinks he announced that he had decided the time was right to see if there was any chance of saving his marriage. He gave his friend a note and asked that it be passed to Lizzie. It read, 'meet me round the pool at once – important.'

Later that afternoon, after receiving the note, Lizzie Gaskin left her home and was never seen alive again. She failed to return home that night, and on the following morning Lizzie's mother went to see Gaskin. He admitted arranging the meeting but claimed that Lizzie had failed to keep the appointment and that he had no idea what had become of her. Her mother then contacted the police and a manhunt was organised but failed to find any trace of the missing woman. Witnesses then told detectives that on the afternoon Lizzie had disappeared they had seen her in the company of her husband walking along Rugeley Road towards woodland at Hednesford Hill. Armed with this new information, on Friday 21 February, detectives questioned Gaskin again and, not satisfied with his answers, held him on suspicion.

The search for Lizzie intensified. Gaskin sat quietly in his cell as more and more officers were deployed to the area to help in the investigation. On Sunday morning it came as something of a surprise to detectives when Gaskin asked to speak to Inspector George Woolley, who was heading the investigation. Gaskin said he wished to help with their enquiries and proceeded to lead officers to a culvert, close to the gas works on Victoria Street. He then pointed to a tank of water surrounding a gasometer, where officers found the butchered body of Lizzie Gaskin.

Her injuries were horrific: not only had Gaskin chopped his wife's head off, but he had ripped open her chest with a knife before a piece of gas pipe had been thrust down the neck, piercing her body like a macabre skewer. Gaskin told officers he had done this to weigh the body down, as he intended to submerge it under water.

At his trial, held before Mr Justice Roche at Stafford Assizes on 11 July, the court heard how Gaskin had met his estranged wife as arranged. Despite her infidelities and the new baby, he asked her to come home and try to make a new start. Instead she refused, but not only that, but she had also told him she was seeking a divorce so she could be free to marry her lover. Gaskin became enraged. He grabbed her by the neck, strangled her, and then concealed her body. Later that night he visited the cinema with his stepbrother, but had left early and made his way back to where he had hidden the body. He then used a wheelbarrow to move the corpse to a place beside the gasworks, where he began dismembering it.

Gaskin's statement describing the moments leading up to his wife's death was told to the court. He said that although his wife had refused his offer to try to save their marriage, she had offered to sleep with him if he went home with her that afternoon. At this he lost his temper, shouting, 'You dare to ask me to go to bed with you, after what you've done?'

Lizzie Gaskin. (Crime Picture Archive)

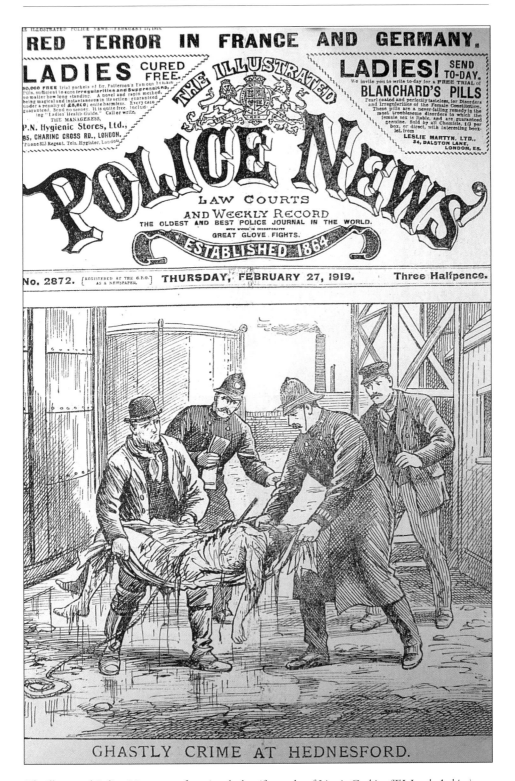

The Illustrated Police News *cover featuring the horrific murder of Lizzie Gaskin. (T.J. Leech Archive)*

A postcard produced to commemorate the murder of Lizzie Gaskin. (T.J. Leech Archive)

He then promised to send her to hell 'where she belonged' and, after dragging her into the woodland, punching her several times, each time emphasising the blows by shouting, 'that's for whoring in London' and 'that's for whoring in Birmingham.'

He then rolled up his sleeve and told her, 'Now I'll tare [sic] your insides out and show it to you' and with that he thrust his arm inside her. As she collapsed in a faint he thrust handfuls of snow inside her, shouting that that should wake her up. He then forced a branch into her mouth, telling her, 'chew on that if you like!'

Gaskin had then told her coldly, 'Listen to me. I am going to kill you and cut you to pieces. He then attacked her with a knife and as she clung to life whimpering slowly, he told her, 'now the devil in hell can have you, I don't want you.' Seeing her still breathing following the horrific disembowelling, he whispered, 'If you get over that we'll say the devil don't want you either.'

With the horrific details of Gaskin's statement read out in court, his counsel chose to focus on this and show that the ferocious nature of the attack was the work of someone insane. While the injuries were clearly the work of a sadist, there was enough of a motive suggested by the prosecution, and confirmed by Gaskin's confession, for the jury to take just thirty-four minutes to convict him of the murder.

Following the decommissioning of certain prisons during the war, Stafford Gaol no longer housed an execution chamber, and as a result Gaskin was taken to Winson Green where, in due course, he kept an 8 o'clock appointment with hangman John Ellis.

14

MOTHERS-IN-LAW

Samuel Westwood, 30 December 1920

George Vaughan feared the worst when his daughter Lydia set out to meet her estranged husband of just six weeks on Saturday night, 11 September 1920.

'Don't go, Liddy,' he pleaded. 'I shall never see you any more until you are a corpse!' They were to be tragically prophetic words.

Lydia Vaughan and Samuel Westwood had married at the end of July. Like many newly-wed young couples – Westwood was 26 years old, she two years his junior – they were unable to afford a place of their own, despite his having a good job as a locksmith at Poole's, close to his family home in Short Heath, Birmingham. While they waited for their own place, they took a room at his parents' home on Bentley Lane.

From the outset this arrangement caused problems; neither set of parents had been keen for the couple to wed, but Westwood's mother in particular soon let her daughter-in-law know her feelings on the marriage. Lydia's parents lived on Cross Street, Spring Bank, Willenhall, and once a week Lydia would return home to see them. On recent visits she had frequently burst into tears, confessing that she was unhappy with the situation at her mother-in-law's.

Lydia's mother, Alice Vaughan, blamed Westwood for not supporting his wife or standing up for her when his mother made some unpleasant remark about Lydia, and she decided it would be best if they split up and for Lydia to come home.

On Monday 6 September Lydia called at her mother's house, again in floods of tears lamenting the position at home.

'I can't put up with it much longer,' she told her mother. 'It's upsetting my nerves.'

This was enough for Alice and she told Lydia she was welcome home whenever she felt like it. Three days later, after her mother-in-law had made another offensive remark, Lydia sent word to her mother, who turned up at the house and helped her daughter gather her things. Westwood stood by silently as she hurriedly packed her bags and returned to Willenhall.

Within hours Lydia seemed to regret her hasty decision and told her mother she wanted to reconcile her differences with her husband and try to salvage their marriage. It was not what her parents wanted as they believed Westwood had a violent nature and, after an earlier quarrel between Westwood and Alice's father, the younger man had made threats that if she left him he would 'kill her and then take his own life.'

On Saturday night, despite her father's voicing his concerns for his daughter's safety, Lydia and her mother made their way to the annual Wake's Fair, held on wasteland off

Walsall Street. Lydia believed her husband would be there and hoped they would be able to work things out. The fairground was crowded and Lydia scanned the queues on the rides and amusements but there was no sign of him and, shortly after 8.30 p.m., she reluctantly made her way home.

Disappointment soon turned to happiness as she spied Westwood making his way up Walsall Street in the direction of the fair. Lydia approached him and, with her mother walking a pace or two behind, they began to talk. Westwood pleaded with his wife to return.

'Come home with me, Liddy,' he implored.

She shook her head and told him, 'I'm sorry, but I can't go back to your mother's. We cannot agree.'

'I'll go into lodgings or anywhere,' Westwood insisted and, sensing that her daughter may have been swayed by his words, Alice Vaughan intervened.

'Lydia, you come home with me tonight,' she said, reaching for her daughter's arm.

Westwood remained calm. 'Well, I'll come for you tomorrow then,' he told her, only for Alice to cut him short, telling Westwood he would need to speak to her husband first.

Suspecting that Lydia's father may also try to dissuade her from returning to him, Westwood flew into a rage. He reached into his jacket, took out his pocketknife and stabbed Lydia once in the neck. He then dropped the knife onto the pavement and, as Alice began to scream and shout, he calmly turned on his heel and hurried in the direction of the local police station.

'Are you a police constable?' he asked as he entered the yard of Walsall Street police station. PC John Brown looked him up and down and replied calmly, 'Yes I am. What do you want?'

'I've just stabbed my wife. She's down the road. I believe I've killed her.'

Westwood was ushered inside, where he was cautioned and detained while other officers hurried back down Walsall Street to where Westwood said he had committed the attack. On the corner of Church Street they found a crowd gathered round the stricken woman, bleeding from a deep cut to the right of her throat. As the officers approached, Lydia's mother handed one of them the bloodstained knife.

Lydia was helped back to the police station and a doctor was summoned, but before Dr Henry Dean arrived Lydia Westwood had died from loss of blood, the cut having severed her jugular vein. In the meantime, Westwood told officers he had swallowed poison. It turned out that he had taken a non-fatal dose of the chemical potassium ferrocyanide, and so Dr Dean administered the prisoner an emetic, causing him to vomit the chemical out of his system.

Westwood was later cautioned and told officers he had drunk two half pints of beer prior to the attack, 'or I could not have done it.' He later added that he had planned to kill his wife from the time she had walked out on him on the previous Thursday.

Samuel Westwood stood trial before Mr Commissioner Hugo Young at Stafford Assizes on 19 November. His defence asked for a verdict of manslaughter and also suggested that the prisoner was insane as a result of head injuries that he had sustained during the First World War.

Westwood had joined the South Staffordshire regiment in 1915 and had seen lots of action in France until finally his unit were sent to Bullecourt in the north of country. Bullecourt was a village on the German Hindenberg Line and on 21 March 1918, during

TRAGEDY AT WILLENHALL "WAKE."

ALLEGED MURDER OF A YOUNG WIFE

EYE-WITNESS'S STORY AT THE INQUEST.

The "wake festival" at Willenhall this year, which is being celebrated as usual with a fair on the grounds in Walsall-street, was marred on Saturday night by the alleged murder of a young married woman.

The deceased is Lydia Westwood, aged 24 years, who on the Saturday before August Bank Holiday, just six weeks ago, married a keysmith named Samuel Westwood, aged 26, who lived at 25, Bentley-lane, Short Heath, with his parents. Like many another couple starting in life, they were faced with the shortage of houses, but the young husband induced his wife to share his parents' home, and she remained there until Thursday last, the 9th inst.

Differences had arisen, and the young woman sent for her mother, with whom she returned to her former home. Her parents are named William and Alice going home with him." Her daughter sadly wanted to speak to her husband, however, as she complained that "they had been scandalising her, and she wanted to have it out."

PRISONER SMILES BEFORE THE MAGISTRATES.

The prisoner, Westwood, was brought before Messrs. S. Lister and J. R. Mattox at Willenhall Police Court on Monday morning, on a charge of murdering his wife by stabbing her with a knife.

He entered the Court smiling, and afterwards turned and scrutinised the large number of persons sitting in the gallery. Observing someone he knew he nodded very familiarly in that direction. He was respectably attired in a grey suit, but wore no collar, his shirt being open at the front. He is of light build, with light wavy hair brushed back from his forehead, and is clean shaven.

Superintendent Tucker informed the Bench that he only intended offering formal evidence to justify a remand.

Sergeant Evans stated that at a few minutes

MRS. LYDIA WESTWOOD.

THE ACCUSED MAN.

A news cutting describing the murder of Lydia Westwood. (T.J. Leech Archive)

a fierce battle, Westwood was rendered unconscious by an exploding shell. When he awoke, he found that he had been taken prisoner by the Germans. He spent the remaining months of the war in a POW camp and although he physically recovered from his injuries, his counsel claimed that mentally he was never the same, frequently losing his temper with little or no provocation.

The prosecution countered this by simply stating it was a crime of passion. Westwood had previously made threats to kill his wife and when, on Saturday night, it became clear she would not be returning home with him that night, he cruelly murdered her before making an unsuccessful attempt to take his own life.

The jury needed just fifteen minutes to reach their verdict, 'guilty of wilful murder', and Westwood was hanged on Thursday 30 December. It was the only time in the twentieth century that three executions took place at three different prisons across the country on the same day.

This unusually large number of capital sentences caused a problem with the prison authorities as the short, official list of executioners contained just five active hangmen and assistants. On duty at Leeds were Tom Pierrepoint and assistant Edward Taylor, whilst long-time assistant William Willis was finally entrusted with the responsibility as a senior executioner at Pentonville, with Robert Baxter engaged as his assistant. This meant that there was no trained man available to act as assistant to John Ellis at Birmingham. This wasn't too much of a problem for the experienced hangman, as during his twenty-year career Ellis had experience of working without an assistant, having done so on one occasion during the First World War when new legislation ruled that assistant hangmen were an unnecessary luxury. Ellis had made his feelings known about this ruling and it was quickly rejected and assistants engaged on subsequent executions. This was the last time that an execution took place in an English prison with no assistant present.

15

'THE LIFE I HAVE HAD TO CONTEND WITH'

Edward O'Connor, 22 December 1921

Well, Lizzie, by the time you get my letter I will have gone to my maker. It is God's will that I leave this world of trials. I am reconciled to that fate and I shall remember you, Lizzie, my wife, and I ask you sometimes to remember me in your prayers. Kiss the children for me. God bless you all. As I think, I hear you as of old, calling: Ted, good-bye.

Last letter penned by Edward O'Connor to his estranged wife.

At 5 a.m. on the morning of Sunday 31 July 1921, 43-year-old Edward O'Connor walked calmly up to police constable Harry Sedgely, who was on duty in Gaol Square, Stafford. He pulled two bloodstained razors from his pocket and offered them to the officer, saying, 'Come on, I'll find you a job. I've killed three or four of my kids with these.'

Sedgely accompanied him back to his house at 7 Sash Street, Stafford, and found four children suffering from terrible throat injuries. All were rushed to the nearby hospital, where three of the young children would subsequently recover. For 5-year-old Thomas O'Connor, help had arrived too late and he was certified dead on arrival.

When O'Connor stood trial before Mr Justice Roche at Stafford Assizes on 16 November, the story behind the tragedy unfolded. Although Edward and Elizabeth O'Connor had eight children, theirs was an unhappy marriage and they frequently quarrelled and fought. He blamed her mother for turning her against him and, perhaps due to this, they had parted a number of times. That summer she had decided to take out a separation order against him under the Married Mothers' Act for wilfully neglecting to maintain his family.

On Monday 25 July, the case was heard and O'Connor was ordered to pay 25s a week for the upkeep of his wife and family. Over the next five days O'Connor called at the house to collect items of clothing and each time they quarrelled as he prepared to leave.

On Saturday morning, 30 July, O'Connor called at the house and, as before, another quarrel broke out. This time, as he made to leave, he lashed out with his fist, striking his wife and bursting her nose. She launched herself at him and they were rolling on the floor fighting and shouting when a neighbour stormed in and dragged him off her.

That night Elizabeth O'Connor did not sleep at the house. Having such a large family, she would often spend the night at her mother's house, across the street at No. 4. After she had given the family their supper, Elizabeth and her 15-year-old daughter Maggie crossed the street to spend the night at No. 4 and left the children in the care of Ellen, Elizabeth's 12-year-old daughter.

Ellen slept in the back bedroom, sharing a bed with 9-year-old Edward and 11-year-old Elizabeth, while in the other bedroom, 7-year-old Mary and 5-year-old Thomas shared one bed, with 3-year-old Bernard having a bed to himself. At shortly before 5 a.m., Ellen was woken by footsteps on the stairs. Her father entered the bedroom and asked where his wife was. 'They are at Granny's,' she told him. In the other room, Bernard, frightened by his father's raised voice, began to cry. Ellen got out of bed and went to comfort him, lifting him out of the bed and holding him in her arms. She then watched in horror as her father approached and, pulling out a razor, ran it across the throats of Mary and Thomas as they lay in their beds. O'Connor then made his way to the back bedroom, where he cut the throats of the other two children. He then calmly pushed past Ellen and Bernard and walked out of the house.

When charged with the murder, O'Connor had showed no remorse, saying only that he had intended to kill his wife because she had taken him to court. He did not deny killing his son, but claimed it was not a wilful act nor had it been premeditated.

His counsel claimed that O'Connor was insane at the time of the killing and referred to the prisoner's statement, made shortly after his arrest, in which he claimed that something had snapped inside him when he found his wife absent from the house.

THE SASH STREET MURDER.

O'Connor Condemned to Death.

ALLEGATION AGAINST RELATIVE.

That two charges of murder affecting Stafford and neighbourhood should appear in the same calendar at the Staffordshire Assizes may be regarded as a remarkable incident in the modern history of the town. Three days this week- Monday, Tuesday, and Wednesday, were occupied, two of them wholly on one case, and partly in the other, in investigating the circumstances of the two crimes. Each case was fully charged with sensational details, though there was not so much fresh matter for public digestion in the

A news cutting of the Sash Street murder. (T.J. Leech Archive)

Although the judge's summing up was fair, his closing statement to the jury made it clear that they could give little consideration to what the defence had said, as the prosecution's argument that it had been a straightforward case of wilful murder had been so strong.

After a short absence, the jury returned to find O'Connor guilty of wilful murder. Asked if he anything to say before sentence was passed, O'Connor stated angrily, 'All I have to say is that my mother-in-law is the sole cause of bringing me to my doom. She is the sole cause of the unhappy state of the life I have had to contend with.'

16

DOMESTIC MATTERS

Elijah Pountney, 11 August 1922

The officer was sympathetic but unable to help, telling the caller at the station, 'The gentleman has broken no law and there is nothing we can do. If you think he is having an affair with your wife that's your business not ours. The police do not get involved in domestic matters.'

Elijah Pountney was at his wit's end. For several weeks he had grown convinced that his wife, Alice, was having an affair with their lodger, Edmund McCann, and that they were planning to take his money and run away together. Pountney could have challenged the other man over the matter, but for the fact that Pountney was 48 years old, small and frail, whilst McCann, several years younger, was a stocky, well-built bricklayer.

On 3 March 1922, in desperation, he had gone to the police, but, while the desk sergeant at Bilston police station understood Pountney's pleas, there was nothing he could do. Pountney told the police that if the situation wasn't resolved, he would be sure to kill his wife. The police did not, it seems, take the threats seriously.

Along with his wife, Pountney had run the Pheasant Inn, Broad Street, Bilston, since 1916, but it was not the thriving hostelry they had hoped for. For one, Pountney was hardly the congenial host, rather he was brusque and rude to customers and, as a result, what few regulars they had tended to be factory workers on lunch breaks, those who called in for a drink on the way home from work, or locals unwilling to find a pub further away from their homes.

To make ends meet they were forced to take in lodgers, while Pountney also took a full time job labouring in the local steel mill, leaving Alice to run the bar during the day. In 1921, Pountney was injured at work when he was accidentally struck on the head with a bag of coal. From then on he suffered headaches, became bad tempered and began to drink heavily, further eating into the slim profits from the pub.

Pountney's bad temper was more often directed at his wife and during one violent quarrel in February 1922, in which he made to strike Alice as she worked behind the bar, McCann leapt to her defence. McCann pulled Pountney away and threatened he would feel his fists if he laid a hand on Alice in future. It was a noble gesture; something any gallant man would probably do when seeing a woman being assaulted, but it was to mark a change in matters at the Pheasant.

Alice now began to look upon McCann as some sort of knight in shining armour. She fussed over him when he returned home from work, made sure he got the choicest cuts of meat at meal times and when he was drinking in the bar, she made sure his glass was always topped up free of charge.

Pountney became convinced that his wife and the lodger were having an affair. Quite why he should have suspected that the younger man would find his dowdy 47-year-old wife attractive never occurred to Pountney and the seeds of suspicion were sown.

On 16 April, Easter Sunday, Alice was in the kitchen with their grown-up son, John, who was helping his mother peel the vegetables for lunch, when Pountney entered. He walked over to Alice and muttered something into her ear, causing her to cry out, 'What, in front of my son?' Pountney then walked out of the kitchen, only to return a few minutes later with long time friend Joe Norton, who had been drinking in the adjacent bar.

Alice told Norton that Pountney had accused her of being pregnant, and that the child she was carrying was McCann's. Pountney then pushed Norton towards Alice, asking, 'Do you want to kiss her, Joe?' Norton stepped back angrily and turned on Pountney, who continued to tell him, 'It'll be the last time anyone does kiss her.'

Once more Pountney left the kitchen only to return moments later and put his arm around his wife. At first it appeared that Pountney was trying to apologise for his actions, but then he seized the knife Alice had been using to cut the vegetables and drew it across her throat.

Alice staggered across the room, blood pouring from a hideous wound. As her son tried to stem the flow, Pountney calmly walked into the hallway, wiped the blood from his hands and left the pub. Pountney headed to a nearby canal where he attempted to drown himself in the murky water. He was however rescued by passers-by and dragged onto the bank, where a policeman gave him first aid. Pountney was then taken to the station, where he was first charged with attempted suicide and later with the wilful murder of his wife.

When he appeared before Mr Justice Shearman at Stafford Assizes on 7 July, Pountney claimed that he had heard Alice and McCann planning to run away together. He claimed she had deliberately favoured the lodger, giving him better meals and free drinks, and that she had also lent him money. Whatever Pountney may have believed, medical evidence revealed that Alice had not been pregnant at the time of her death.

His counsel suggested he was insane, claiming that the headaches and mood swings he had suffered since the accident at work, coupled with heavy drinking and worries over his wife's alleged adultery, had unhinged Pountney's mind. Unfortunately for the defence, Pountney had been heard to make threats against his wife by a number of people, including the officer who had informed him the police did not get involved in domestic matters. This, the prosecution claimed, was proof of premeditation; the jury concurred and Pountney was found guilty as charged.

17

THE BIGAMIST

William Rider, 18 December 1922

William Rider was keeping a little secret from his bride-to-be. As they exchanged vows at Harbury parish church, Warwickshire, in February 1918, the 36-year-old window cleaner and chimney sweep had neglected to mention to his new wife that, technically at least, he was still a married man. True, he had separated from his wife and had custody of their children, but he was not the widower she believed him to be. Although his wife had walked out and left him several years before, legally he was still a married man. The marriage ceremony they went through was, therefore, unlawful.

The new Mrs Rider was 20-year-old Rosilla 'Rose' Patience Barton, a war widow who had lost her first husband in 1916. The attractive young woman, some sixteen years Rider's junior, had captivated him and, following their marriage, they moved into a house at 2 Elborrow Street, Rugby. Relations between the two soon began to deteriorate. Rider had a violent temper and often took it out on his new wife. Rose eventually walked out and returned to her mother's at Harbury. She did this several times during the next four years, but each time Rider was able to persuade her to come home, after promising he would change his ways.

Things changed in the spring of 1921, when Rachael Freeman, Rose's mother, learned that Rider already had a wife when he had married her daughter. She asked Rose's 16-year-old sister, Harriet, to break the news. Rider was soon able to reassure his wife that while he may have kept his marriage a secret, it was long dead except on paper. This revelation seemed to have done nothing to harm the relationship and a short time later Harriet was invited to move in with her sister and brother-in-law in Rugby.

Relations between the young girl and her brother-in-law quickly became intense. Rider began a secret affair with Harriet and, the following summer, she found herself pregnant. Harriet confessed to her mother and, although it caused a dreadful scene with lots of angry words and threats, Rider was somehow able to smooth things over and salvage his marriage.

On 25 August, Rose and her husband travelled to Harbury to visit her family for the day. On the following day, Rider and Harriet disappeared. Believing they had eloped, a search was mounted which drew a blank, and nothing was heard from either Rider or the young girl until Wednesday 6 September, when a tearful Harriet reappeared at her mother's. She denied she had absconded with Rider, but the family deemed it too much of a coincidence and, although she was welcomed back into the family, the proverbial knives were out for Rider. When he heard threats had been made against him he decided to take matters into his own hands.

MURDERER AND HIS VICTIM. FROM A REC[
PHOTOGRAPH.

William Rider and his bigamous bride. (T.J. Leech Archive)

On the following morning, Thursday 7 September, Rose Rider woke to find her husband standing at the foot of her bed. In his hands he was cradling a sixteen-bore shotgun, which he pointed at Rose.

'Oh Bill, don't!' she cried, but Rider pulled the trigger and blasted her in the head, killing her instantly. The shot brought Rose's mother into the room and she began to grapple with Rider and managed to disarm him. She noticed that Rider was barefoot and after saying that he meant her no harm, he went downstairs, fastened his boots and left the house. Rider was arrested later that morning at nearby Leamington. He told detectives that he had accidentally shot his wife and said he had been on his way to surrender when he had been apprehended.

At his trial on 17 November before Mr Justice Lush at Warwick Assizes, Rider maintained the shooting was accidental. The prosecution called on a number of witnesses, who swore they had heard Rider make threats and physically abuse his wife. Rider could offer no plausible reason as to why he had entered the bedroom carrying a loaded gun and this ultimately told against him, with the jury taking just a short time to find him guilty.

THE BEDROOM MURDER AT HARBURY.

Rider's Stealthy Entrance Dramatically Described.

HALF - SISTER'S COURAGEOUS CONDUCT.

Girl Refuses to Answer Questions.

ACCUSED MAN'S MATRIMONIAL MUDDLE.

A verdict of "Wilful murder" was last Saturday returned by a coroner's jury at Harbury against William Rider (40), the Rugby window cleaner who shot Rosilla Patience Borton (24), with whom he had been living after, as alleged, contracting a bigamous marriage with her.

Police Court proceedings were begun on Friday and continued on Monday, but only formal evidence was given, and the accused is in custody pending further investigations. He will be brought up again next Monday at Southam.

INQUEST REVELATIONS.

THE PRISONER LISTENS TO THE EVIDENCE.

The accused man was present in the custody of police constables at the inquest, which was held on Saturday at the Dog Inn, Harbury. He was brought handcuffed to a police constable, Superintendent Jackson and Inspector Scott having also come with him from Southam. His arrival was witnessed by a large number of villagers, who had assembled together, and their number increased to several hundred while the inquest was in progress, the crowd remaining to see Rider driven away in a motor-car in charge of the police.

Before the inquest Rider had stated he desired to give evidence, but, acting upon found that he wasn't there, neither was her daughter Harriet, and she saw nothing of either until September 6th.

Mrs. Freeman afterwards said Rider later and told him she was going to Harbury, but Rider replied that if she told him that again he would cut her throat with a razor. On the night of the 6th instant, Harriet returned home and said she had been to Harbury, but did not mention Rider. Witness took care to lock up the doors and fasten the windows, as she had heard Rider was about, and was frightened in consequence of his threats.

PRECAUTIONS AT HOME.

Witness slept with Minnie and Harriet (two of her daughters) that night, and Rose slept in another bed with another daughter in the same room, which was the back bedroom. In the front bedroom were two other beds, which were occupied by other members of the family. Her sons went off to work at 6 a.m., and Florrie, who worked at the Old New Inn, went up at 7.10 a.m. At the bottom of the stairs Florrie said to her, "Mother, I am just going out; you had better fasten the door." Having heard that Rider was about, witness went down and locked the door at 7.20 a.m., and returned to bed. The deceased was then awake and said she thought she heard someone tapping the door. Mrs. Freeman continued and it is quite easy for you to do so. Make up your mind quickly. I can't keep the jury waiting.

The witness made no answer, and the Coroner then said: "Take, this witness away for contempt of court."

Inspector Scott (to a constable): Keep her in custody.

The witness was led away sobbing.

A COURAGEOUS WOMAN.

Mrs. Edith Elizabeth Large, another married daughter of Mrs. Freeman, wife of Arthur Thomas Large, living near to the house where deceased was shot, said that Minnie, aged 13, ran to their house had seen William Rider and that he had a gun in his hand, and was going to shoot Rose.

Witness got straight out of bed, put on her boots and went round to the house in her night attire. She went upstairs and saw her mother bending over the deceased's bed. Rider was holding the deceased's hand. He said "Have I killed her?" She replied "Yes, you have; she's dead." The prisoner wanted to kiss the deceased, but Mrs. Freeman prevented him.

Witness went round home, and her husband went to Bishops Itchington for the policeman. After putting some more

Rider's crime made the headlines of the local papers. (T.J. Leech Archive)

18

OVER MONEY

John Fisher, 5 January 1926

It was one of the most remarkable episodes in the history of British execution. The condemned man, described by the hangman as a pale-faced, diminutive creature, standing just 5ft 3in in height and weighing barely 138lbs, was led across the frost-covered prison yard to the scaffold in a daze, his footsteps faltering as he stumbled the last few paces into the execution chamber and onto the wooden trapdoors. To prevent him collapsing on the drop, the two warders assigned to watch over the condemned man's last moments, stood close to the prisoner as the assistant executioner secured the prisoner's ankles.

Executioner William Willis, a veteran of almost a hundred executions in his twenty-year career as both hangman and assistant, whipped the white cap out of his pocket and, in his haste to carry out the execution with alacrity, tried to place it over the head of the warder, who was standing much closer to the condemned man than was usual. The mistake was noticed just as the white cloth hood was about to cover the warder's head and, realising his error, Willis swiftly returned to his prisoner and covered his head before placing the noose and darting to the lever. As the drop crashed open and the man died, the prison officer realised he had almost become the victim. At the speed in which a twentieth-century executioner worked, with hangings timed in seconds, if the hangman had placed the hood over the guard, the noose would have followed within seconds and in all probability an innocent man would have been hanged.

John Fisher was a 58-year-old machinist who kept an immaculately maintained terrace house at 1 Back 27 Wright Street, Small Heath, Birmingham, with 56-year-old Mrs Ada Taylor, his partner of the last fourteen years, and Jessie Dutton, Ada's married daughter who lodged with them. Although a kindly, well-liked and immensely house-proud man, who had separated from his wife many years before, Fisher was not hardworking and had been out of any sort of regular employment for over three years. In order to make ends meet, Fisher often borrowed money from both Ada and Jessie, which he seldom, if ever, repaid.

It was an argument over money which had broken out on the afternoon of Sunday 25 October. Ada discovered that Fisher had pawned a tablecloth which belonged to her, and they exchanged words. Jessie Dutton had been sitting in the lounge opposite Fisher, while Ada busied herself doing the housework, when the quarrel had broken out. Jessie seemed to sense that something was amiss and, slipping on her coat, she left the house. It was an act that probably saved her life.

Hangman William Willis caused a remarkable incident at Fisher's execution. (Author's collection)

Returning later that night, Jessie was surprised to find the front door locked. She let herself in and, after looking in a couple of the rooms, found her mother seemingly asleep in bed, with the bedclothes pulled up over her head. Receiving no reply to her calling, Jessie pulled back the sheets and found her mother lying dead in a pool of blood, her throat cut.

At almost the same moment as the body of Ada Taylor was discovered by her daughter, two policemen boarded a tramcar in Small Heath. One of them, PC Charles Bent, was walking along the top deck when one of the passengers stopped him and declared, 'I've done a murder in Wright Street. I want to give myself up to you.'

Taken to the police station, the passenger gave his name as John Fisher and admitted that he had killed a woman that afternoon. Fisher told detectives he had stabbed a woman and had then washed the knife, tidied up the house and closed the door behind him. He said he had spent the afternoon wandering the streets, during which time Ada's body lay in the house undiscovered, before boarding a tram and confessing to the first policeman he came upon.

At his trial before Mr Justice Talbot at Warwick Assizes on 4 December, John Fisher pleaded insanity and confessed that he had planned to kill both women in the house. The court heard Fisher calmly testify that at dinner time on the day of the murder, he had sharpened all the knives, as he usually did on a Sunday afternoon, but had purposely kept one of them back. His defence, based on the fact Fisher had been discharged from the army as an epileptic, failed.

NOTE
Hangman William Willis referred to the case of John Fisher in his memoirs, published in the *Sunday Dispatch* under the heading 'They nearly hanged a warder by mistake'

shortly before his death in 1939. In his account it stated that the prisoner's height and weight were 5ft 3ins and 138lbs. Willis's account was edited by a newspaper reporter, with the assistance of crime historian Dr Harold Dearden, and was based on information contained in Willis's diary, a copy of which was photographed in the newspaper account. Despite this, the official prison LPC4 sheet shows that Fisher's details were listed as 5ft 5½ins tall and 144lbs in weight.

19

SMALL GRIEVANCES

George Sharpes, 13 April 1926

George Sharpes had had a troubled up bringing. A petty thief with low intelligence, he was soon in trouble with the authorities for a number of minor misdemeanours and, following his arrest for breaking into a church at Crewe, he was sentenced to four years in a reform school. On his release from the Cheshire borstal, Sharpes was offered a job on a farm at Crewe, run by Arthur Crabtree, a gentleman farmer. He soon settled down to life on the farm, and impressed his employers with his willingness to work hard. When the family purchased a new farm at Ladbroke, near Southam, Warwick, they invited Sharpes, now aged 19, to come and live with them.

Arthur Crabtree had always been careful to make no mention of the young lad's past, but within days of their arriving to run the farm, a cowman learned about his background and word soon spread amongst the other workers on the farm. Sharpes had been befriended by Crabtree's wife, Milly, a very attractive woman and, at 25 years old, several years younger than her husband.

She was sympathetic when Sharpes became upset about the revelations of his past and encouraged him when he told her he intended to apply for a work permit in Canada. This idea was dashed when Sharpes was informed that no one with a criminal record would be considered suitable for Canadian citizenship. Reluctantly, Sharpes had to forget the notion of emigrating and settled back into work on the farm, where he was happy enough until he was suddenly informed he would have to find lodgings away from the farm. To compensate for his upheaval, he was given a wage increase, but it was still barely enough to live on.

Sharpes was now angry at the fact he was being gossiped about by his workers, whom he thought mistrusted him because of his past; he was angry that his chance to emigrate had been refused, and the cost of his new lodgings meant he was always short of money. He was also angry at what he felt was a poor wage for the hours he was expected to work. He had by this time also discovered that it was Milly Crabtree

George Sharpes was hanged a few days after
his twentieth birthday. (Author's collection)

Sharpes's victim, Milly Crabtree.
(T.J. Leech Archive)

who had told workmates about his past. It was therefore Mrs Crabtree whom he now blamed for all his woes.

On Wednesday morning, 13 January 1926, Arthur Crabtree left the farm and travelled to Cheshire on business. Sharpes was at work on the farm, carrying out some general repairs around the farmhouse. In the afternoon he was carrying out some carpentry when Mrs Crabtree passed by him. She was in and out of the house on a number of occasions and the more he saw her, the angrier he became. Finally, as she walked by him again, he picked up a hammer, swung it around and struck her on the head.

Satisfied that Milly Crabtree was dead, Sharpes took out a knife from his toolbox and tried to cut his own throat. Unable to take his own life, he went into the kitchen where he knew there was a cupboard containing poison. He uncorked the bottle and drank from it, but before the poison had time to take effect, 10-year-old Kathleen Coleman, Mary's stepdaughter, discovered Sharpes lying on the floor. 'Never mind me, go down to the missus. I have killed her,' he said and workers came running after hearing her screams. Soon both were taken to hospital; Milly Crabtree was already dead on arrival, but Sharpes was nursed back to health and was soon well enough to stand trial for murder.

At Warwickshire Assizes before Mr Justice Shearman on 9 March, Sharpes made no attempt to deny the crime. He admitted he had been angry at Mrs Crabtree for revealing his past and at the poor wages he received from his employers.

His defence claimed that Sharpes was insane, but although doctors found that he was broody and emotional, there was nothing in his behaviour to suggest insanity. Summing up, Mr Justice Shearman focused on the medical evidence and said that it was not for Harley Street to give verdicts of guilty or not guilty: that was for the jury to decide. 'Because a man was of small intelligence and was excited at small grievances, it was not the law that he could knock out someone's brains and then say, "Oh, but I am

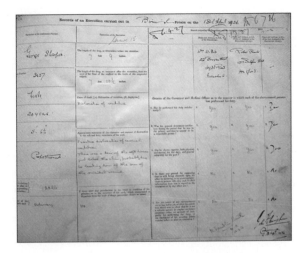

The LPC4 for George Sharpes. (Author's collection)

not normal." In this case the jury have to consider whether the man was normal. Very few criminals were normal!'

The jury took just thirty minutes to find Sharpes guilty of wilful murder. While awaiting the hangman he made a statement to the governor in which he said he believed if he had been birched in his early years, it may have frightened him into giving up a life of crime. George Sharpes was hanged just fourteen days after his twentieth birthday.

20

THE IMPOSTER

James Joseph Power, 31 January 1928

It was shortly before 10 p.m. on Saturday, 2 July 1927, when 20-year-old Olive Turner and her boyfriend Charles Broomhead left the cinema on Winson Green Road, close to Birmingham Gaol. It being a warm, balmy night, they decided on a leisurely stroll home and headed for the nearby canal. It was a popular spot with courting couples and as they walked hand-in-hand along the towpath a man approached, telling them he was a plain-clothes policeman and that they were trespassing on private property. He asked them their names and, when they told him, he asked for proof of their identities.

When they were unable to provide any, the man told them he was taking them into custody.

As they headed up the canal side, they passed other courting couples and Olive turned to ask why he was not arresting them as well. 'Two will do for me,' said the man, maintaining his brisk pace. The man then slowed down and turned to the couple, telling them they could 'square it with him'. Broomhead searched his pockets, knowing he had nothing but a few coppers, and offered him four pennies.

'Four pence is no good to me,' the man scorned.

The couple had by now realised the man wasn't a police officer and, sensing they may be in danger, Broomhead told Olive to make a run for it. She turned on her heels and headed up the footpath towards a couple, who stood cuddling against a fence. As Olive raced away, the bogus policeman gave chase, followed closely by Charles Broomhead.

Broomhead caught up with the man and tried to pull him back, only to feel the force of a punch to the jaw that sent him dazed to the floor. By the time he regained his senses, both Olive and the man had disappeared. He rushed to Olive's home in case she had made it back there and, when he found she hadn't, he called upon members of her family to help look for her. The search drew a blank and the police were notified. By daybreak Olive's body had been discovered floating in the canal. She was transferred to a local hospital where a post-mortem found death was due to drowning.

Broomhead himself was, initially, the main suspect, but once police interviewed people who had been on the canal bank that night, his story tallied and investigations into finding the real killer were stepped up. One witness, who had been with his girlfriend on the footpath, told officers that at 11.30 p.m. he had spoken to a man dragging the distressed girl by the waist. The man told him he was a policeman taking her into custody. Five minutes later, another couple said they had heard the sound of a struggle in the darkness, which was followed by a splash.

All the witnesses claimed they would recognise the man again. The descriptions given, and the fact that the man was impersonating a police officer, led detectives to speak to James Joseph Power, a 33-year-old former policeman who had been discharged from the police service in 1922 after being accused of assaulting a maid while on duty. Power lived in nearby Heath Green Road and was taken in for questioning. He was identified by Charles Broomhead and several others who had been on the canal towpath.

Power simply claimed they were all mistaken and that he had not been anywhere near the canal on the day in question. He stood trial before Mr Justice Swift at Birmingham Assizes in December. The prosecution counsel, Sir Norman Birkett, based his case on the positive identification by the witnesses on the canal bank, but Power insisted he had been drinking in a public house and had gone home at 10.30 p.m. He said he had not left the house again that night.

On 9 December, following a two-day trial, he was found guilty and when passing sentence, the judge addressed the prisoner, saying, 'For the crime of which the jury has found you guilty, our law knows but one punishment and that punishment is death.'

'I quite understand that,' Power replied. 'I don't want any sympathy from you.'

As the sentenced finished with a solemn 'Amen', Power turned to the judge in one last touch of defiance and said, 'I will appeal against the sentence you know.'

Olive Turner. (TNA: PRO)

The canal bank where Olive Turner met her death, in the shadow of Winson Green Gaol. (TNA: PRO)

letter should be

CRETARY OF STATE,
E OFFICE,
LONDON, S.W. 1.
g number quoted:—

HOME OFFICE,

WHITEHALL.

514893/4.

27th January, 1928.

Sir,

I am directed by the Secretary of State to acquaint you that, having had under his consideration the case of James Joseph Power, now lying under sentence of death in Birmingham Prison, he has failed to discover any sufficient ground to justify him in advising His Majesty to interfere with the due course of law.

I am,

Sir,

Your obedient Servant,

E. Blackwell

The Acting Chairman of
the Prison Commissioners.

The letter stating that Power's execution would go ahead as planned. (Author's collection)

Crowds congregate outside the prison gates as Power is executed. (Crime Picture Archive)

At the appeal, the defence counsel first tried to discredit the testimony of the witnesses and also claimed that even if Power had carried off Olive, there was no proof that he was responsible for her death. The counsel suggested that although Power may well have assaulted and robbed her, she might have fallen into the canal accidentally. This had already been refuted by medical evidence, which found there was no water in the woman's stomach, suggesting she was probably unconscious when she entered the water. The appeal failed.

Following conviction, it was reported that Power had often preyed on young couples on the tow path, threatening them with arrest unless they gave him money, or, in some cases, if the woman would perform a sex act on him.

In what was a busy month for executions across the country, he would be the tenth person hanged in January. Power walked to the scaffold at Winson Green on 31 January 1928, just a stone's throw from where he had committed the brutal murder.

21

PARTNERS IN CRIME

Victor Edward Betts, 3 January 1931

The job had been carefully planned. They had watched a number of times as the old man went about his regular routine of walking to the National Provincial Bank at Six Ways, banking the takings from William Taylor & Co., drapers, of Potters Hill, Aston, Birmingham, and, when his appearance at the bank could be anticipated almost to the minute, they decided it was time to put their plan into action.

Sixty-three-year-old William Thomas Andrews had worked for Taylor & Co. for over thirty years, and had risen to the position of head porter. It was his responsibility to see that the wages were collected and takings deposited at the bank on a daily basis. At just after 2 p.m. on Monday 21 July 1930, Andrews collected a bag with the weekend's takings of just over £900, along with the paying-in book, and set out on the five-minute walk to the bank. It was a journey he would never complete.

Earlier that lunchtime, two 21-year-olds, Victor Betts and Herbert Ridley, had called into Rose Garage on Park Road and arranged to hire a yellow Morris Cowley four-seat saloon. Coal merchant Thomas Young of Holte Road owned the car and, after the youths told him they wanted it for an hour or so to take an elderly relative across the city, they agreed on a price and Ridley signed the hire agreement.

It had been Betts who had first hit on the idea of robbing the old man. He was unemployed and eking out a meagre living as a street gambler when he noticed Andrews carrying his bag of money to the bank. When he saw him a second and then a third time

A car is positioned on the corner of Victoria Road and Rifle Crescent for this police scene of crime photograph. (TNA: PRO)

over the coming days, he discussed his plans with a number of his criminally-inclined friends before settling on lorry driver Ridley, the only one of his friends who could drive. This was an essential part of his plan.

That afternoon, with Ridley at the wheel of their hire car, they parked up on the corner of Victoria Road and Rifle Crescent, adjacent to the bank, and waited. When Betts saw Andrews approach he climbed out and hid around the corner. As the man passed him, Betts struck him on the head and pushed him to the ground. He then snatched the bag and, as the car screeched up alongside, he tossed it into the back and climbed into the front seat as Ridley sped away.

Van driver Charles Dowd was driving down Victoria Road when he saw the attack. At the same moment a yellow car had pulled up and the assailant climbed in. As it sped off he attempted to give chase but soon lost it as it reached the Six Ways junction. Dowd was able to give a good description of the car and it was quickly traced to Rose Garage, where detectives learned that it had been hired by Ridley. Officers hurried to his rooms on Barton Street, but found he had already absconded. The car was later found abandoned, the bag lying empty on the back seat. Officers had by now also learned the identity of Ridley's accomplice and, with Andrews lying in hospital with a fractured skull sustained in the fall, a hunt for his attackers began. The hunt for the thieves became a murder enquiry when Andrews died from his injuries three days later. He never regained consciousness.

It was almost two weeks later before detectives had the attackers in custody. On Sunday 6 August a car was involved in an accident in Sussex. There had been four people in the car, two young men and two women, when it ran into a ditch and, when officers went to follow up the incident at an address the men had given, they found a link with the murder in Birmingham.

The enquiry then focused on the south coast, and on the following Tuesday night Ridley was picked up in Brighton. When searched, he was found to be carrying over

MURDER HUE AND CRY.

POLICE SCOUR COUNTRY FOR CAR BANDITS.

Sequel to Messenger's Fate.

("News of the World" Special.)

Detectives up and down the country yesterday kept a sharp look-out for two young men whom the police are anxious to trace as suspects in a sensational bandit outrage at Aston, Birmingham.

Descriptions of the pair have been circulated to every police-station, and, armed with these vital particulars, officers in London and provincial centres yesterday carried out special searches of haunts likely to be used by fugitives as places of concealment.

So extensive and thorough is the hue and cry on foot that it seems impossible that the two individuals can escape detection for any length of time.

An outrageous attack on a middle-aged man who, in broad daylight, was robbed of a bag containing £908, and left dying on the pavement, gave rise to the present search.

The victim's skull was fractured by a blow with some weapon which the police have not yet been able to discover.

ROBBED AND LEFT DYING.

AMAZING OUTRAGE IN DAYLIGHT.

REWARD FOR INFORMATION OF SUSPECTS.

(FROM OUR OWN CORRESPONDENT.)

was ordered at the ports to prevent the men from getting away out of the country was maintained, and a close surveillance was kept at the principal railway termini in London.

The police are hopeful that rewards which are offered will be helpful in the search. The Chief Constable of Birmingham offered a reward of £30 for information leading to the arrest of the men. A further £100 reward is offered by the dead man's employers, Messrs. Taylor and Sons.

The murder of William Andrews made the headlines of newspapers across the country. (Author's collection)

£150 in cash. Betts was picked up later that night and when officers searched their rooms at Grand Parade they found another £250. Taken into custody and brought back to Birmingham, both men admitted being involved in the robbery but, from the outset, Ridley maintained he had merely driven the getaway car.

Their two-day murder trial before Mr Commissioner Mitchell-Innes at Warwickshire Assizes began on 4 December. In the case of Ridley, his defence maintained that he had only been the driver of the car. He said that when they planned the robbery, Betts had

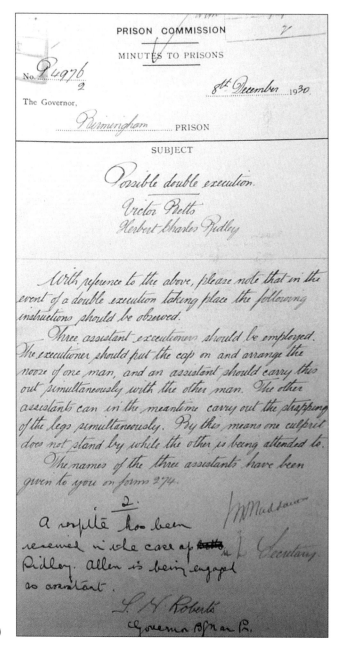

Plans were underway for a rare double execution at Birmingham before Betts was reprieved. (Author's collection)

told him he simply planned to push Andrews to the ground and snatch the bag. Ridley claimed that had he known Betts intended to use violence he would have taken no part in the crime.

Betts' defence was that he had not intended to kill Andrews and therefore he was only guilty of manslaughter. Betts said he had used minimal force and his counsel produced medical evidence to show that Andrews had an abnormally thin skull. Despite this, the prosecution claimed it was a brutal attack on an innocent man going about his business and that both had undertaken the attack and, while Ridley may have claimed to have merely acted as the driver in the actual crime, he had been a willing accomplice and had received an equal share of the spoils. Having considered their verdict, the jury returned to find Betts guilty of murder and, as Ridley had been party to the common design, they found him equally guilty. Both were sentenced to death and each immediately launched an appeal.

The partners in crime would not hang side by side, although preparations were well underway for what would be a rare double execution at the gaol. Just days before the sentences were due to be carried out, the Home Secretary announced that Ridley's appeal had been successful. Spared the gallows, he was sentenced instead to life imprisonment. There was to be no such mercy for Victor Betts, the mastermind behind the crime and the man who had yielded the fatal blow. He walked to the gallows on a frosty and foggy Saturday morning in January 1931. Herbert Charles Ridley would serve just five years before being released on licence in December 1935.

22

JERRY'S REVENGE

Jeremiah Hanbury, 2 February 1933

'I cannot remember anything ... I don't know if she cut my throat or I cut hers ... that's all I know about it.'

Statement by Jeremiah Hanbury following his arrest for murder.

Jeremiah Hanbury had been friends with James and Jessie Payne for several years and was a frequent visitor to their home at 11 The Leys, Newtown Brockmore, near Brierley Hill. Forty-nine-year-old Hanbury was a widower and had worked as a foundry puddler before becoming unemployed. Sometime in the summer of 1929, Hanbury began a secret affair with 39-year-old Mrs Payne, a mother of four young children. At the end of July 1932, Jessie suddenly told Hanbury she wanted to end the affair. He took the news badly and made a number of requests for her to change her mind, but she refused.

Hanbury suspected he had been replaced in Jessie's bed by another man, Bert Eardley. He told Jessie's husband that his wife was being unfaithful and, although Jessie admitted to her husband she had had sex with Hanbury, she claimed that he had forced himself on her. When Payne confronted Hanbury about this, he denied the claims, saying that he had often paid Jessie for sex and suspected that Eardley was now doing the same.

On Monday afternoon, 17 October, Hanbury called at the house and, finding Jessie alone, he struck her two blows with a hammer, knocking her unconscious. He then picked up a razor and cut her throat so severely that she was almost decapitated. After making an attempt to cut his own throat, Hanbury staggered out into the street muttering, 'Jerry said revenge; Jerry's had revenge.' A large crowd watched as he staggered down the road, where he soon gave himself up to a policeman.

At his trial before Mr Justice Humphreys at Birmingham Assizes on 8 December, it was suggested that Hanbury, although hard-working and of previous good character, was unstable at times and inclined to be quarrelsome. There was no doubt he was guilty, but was he insane at the time of the crime as he claimed at his arrest when he told officers he could not remember anything of the events of that afternoon?

The body of Jessie Payne on her living room floor. (TNA: PRO)

Number 11 The Leys, Newtown Brockmore, where Jessie Payne was murdered by Jeremiah Hanbury. (TNA: PRO)

His counsel told the court that when a previous relationship had ended bitterly, Hanbury had tried to kill himself, and there was also a history of insanity in the family. As a result, he became depressed and it was during this depression he had committed the crime.

As Hanbury awaited his fate in the condemned cell at Winson Green, events were taking place that would herald the career of one of the most well-known executioners of the twentieth century. Albert Pierrepoint, nephew of the country's chief executioner, Tom Pierrepoint, had recently graduated through the executioners' training school at London's Pentonville Prison. Before he could be entrusted with undertaking his duties as an assistant executioner, he was required to attend an execution as a non-participating witness. The young Pierrepoint had been offered several jobs, each of which had ended with the prisoners' being granted a reprieve and, when this happened twice over the Christmas period, it was decided to ask Governor Ball if Pierrepoint could be present at the execution of Hanbury. The memo specifically stated that he was to play no active part. Request granted, Pierrepoint arrived at the prison on Wednesday afternoon on 1 February 1933 in the company of his uncle.

Albert Pierrepoint makes mention of this case in his autobiography, in which he refers to the prisoner as Gerald Hutchins. He said that the prison officers, who all called him 'Jerry', had treated him with courtesy and respect. Pierrepoint recalled that he had arrived at the prison just as Hanbury's relatives had left and the prison officer, who was present at the farewell interview, said that the prisoner had told his sister to pull down the blind on the kitchen window at a moment before eight o'clock on the following morning, the time of the execution. He asked her to release it as the clock struck the

Albert Pierrepoint was present at the execution of Jerry Hanbury as a non-participating witness. (Author's collection)

Jerry Hanbury. (Author's collection)

The LPC4 for Jerry Hanbury, showing Albert Pierrepoint present for instruction only. (Author's collection)

hour and to think of 'poor old Jerry'. Pierrepoint states in the book that he had come to an arrangement with assistant Robert Wilson, allowing him to take an active part in the execution, but official reports clearly show that this was not the case and he only witnessed proceedings.

Hanbury spent his last hours singing loudly in his cell and asked the governor for a large breakfast of bacon and eggs, claiming he needed energy because he was about to embark on a long journey.

He smiled at the guards as the hangmen entered the cell, and, as his arms were strapped, he told them to be good before turning to the governor and thanking him for the trouble he had gone to on his behalf.

23

THE KILLER WITH SIZE FOUR SHOES

Stanley Eric Hobday, 28 December 1933

In the early hours of Sunday, 27 August 1933, an intruder forced an entry into 8 Moor Street, West Bromwich. As he removed a pane of glass, it slipped from his fingers and smashed, alerting the occupants who were sleeping upstairs. Gladys Fox roused her 24-year-old husband, Charles. At his wife's insistence that he go investigate, Fox lit a candle and, dressed in just his underwear, he went downstairs. As he opened the door at the bottom of the stairs, his wife waited anxiously on the landing. No sooner had Fox reached the bottom of the stairs than the candle was extinguished and in the darkness a scuffle took place. Fox staggered upstairs and collapsed on the bedroom floor with a knife embedded in his back. He had been stabbed several times and died from his wounds within minutes.

When detectives examined the murder scene, they found a set of footprints in the soil outside the house and spots of blood, which didn't match those of the victim, and which had more than likely come from a cut the killer had sustained whilst gaining entry through the window. Casts were made of the prints, which were of size four shoes, suggesting the killer was either a child or an adult with unusually small feet.

As officers continued their investigations, they learned of two other crimes that had taken place in the area that night. At the first someone had broken into a butcher's shop on Bromford Lane. Here, the intruder had had the audacity to help himself to a meal, drink a bottle of milk, then wash and shave in the sink before repairing his clothing with a needle and cotton. A thief had also broken into a garage close by, belonging to Mrs Winifred Randle, and had stolen her Javelin Jowett motorcar.

Number 8 Moor Street, West Bromwich. (TNA: PRO)

Charles Fox. (T.J. Leech Archive)

Winifred Randle's Javelin Jowett, recovered by police from a ditch in Cheshire. (TNA: PRO)

The intruder at the butcher's shop had left a similar set of diminutive footprints, but more tellingly was a clear set of fingerprints on the milk bottle, which led police to Stanley Eric Hobday, a 21-year-old electrician who lived on nearby Sam's Lane. Hobday was already known to the police as a petty thief, having served a number of sentences in reform school and borstal for petty larceny and housebreaking.

Later that night the stolen car was recovered in Cheshire. The driver had been speeding down High Lane, Winsford, some seventy miles north of West Bromwich, when he had lost control of the vehicle and it turned onto its roof. The car also had Hobday's fingerprints on the steering wheel and a suitcase in the back of the car bore Hobday's initials.

Detectives examined the knife used to commit the murder. It carried a distinctively coloured handle and had been manufactured by Clarke & Sons, of Sheffield. It was a limited edition model, with fewer than twenty of this design produced. When a description of the knife was published in a newspaper, a young boy came forward to say that shortly before the murder he had been camping in a field next to a man who had used a similar knife. Shown a photograph, he identified the camper as Stanley Hobday.

Although the case had featured heavily in the national press, detectives then chose to make the historic step of asking the BBC to appeal for information on the whereabouts of Hobday over the wireless. Listeners throughout the country became alerted to the manhunt and, after a number of false sightings, a farm worker spotted a man he thought might be the fugitive. Detectives responded quickly and detained the man at Rockcliffe, close to Gretna Green. The manhunt had lasted three days.

Returned back to West Bromwich, Hobday's jacket was found to have been repaired with the black cotton from the house at Newton, and on his arm, beneath the tear, was a freshly healed cut. Casts made of Hobday's footprints matched those left at the murder scene and, satisfied they had their man, detectives charged him with murder.

Hobday's defence when he appeared before Mr Justice Talbot at Staffordshire Assizes on 14 November was that although he admitted he had broken into the butcher's shop, he was not the man who had broken into Charles Fox's home and committed the murder.

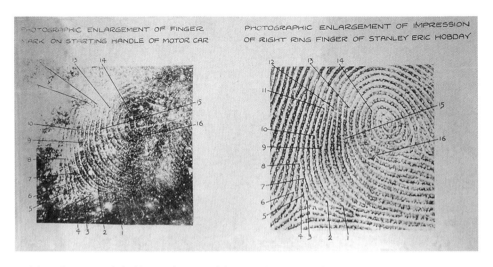

Hobday's fingerprints linked him to the scene of the crime. (TNA: PRO)

Casts of the footprints found at 8 Moor Street. (TNA: PRO)

His defence counsel asked the jury if they believed a man could commit a murder, then travel a few hundred yards to a shop where, after breaking in, he had washed, shaved, calmly thread a needle to repair a rip in his jacket, then helped himself to food and drink before driving off in a stolen car knowing full well that there would be police in the area by then.

The prosecution claimed the case against the accused was strong: Hobday's fingerprints were at the butcher's shop, as were the size four footprints, which the killer had left at the scene of the murder.

Attempts were made by the defence to discredit the footprint evidence by suggesting that the prints in the yard were not an exact match to Hobday's. However, if the footprints weren't an exact match to Hobday's shoes, they were still those of a man with size four shoes, a very unusual size for an adult male. Coupled with this was the evidence of the knife, which a witness had testified to seeing in the possession of Hobday a few days before the murder.

Hobday was found guilty after a three-day trial, and two separate petitions were gathered asking for his reprieve, one based on his mental health claiming he was a 'moral imbecile' suffering from epilepsy. Neither swayed the Home Secretary, who wrote that he saw no grounds for interference with the sentence, and three days after Christmas Hobday's size four shoes were lined up against the chalk mark on the trapdoors and the hangman pulled the lever, sending him to his death.

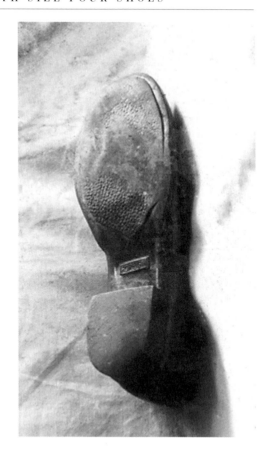

Hobday's size 4 shoes. (TNA: PRO)

Stanley Eric Hobday. (T.J. Leech Archive)

Hobday's execution as featured in the Illustrated Police News. *(T.J. Leech Archive)*

24

'NURSE' WADDINGHAM

Dorothea Nancy Waddingham, 16 April 1936

Following the death of her husband of eight years, Thomas Willoughby Leech, in 1930, mother of three, 30-year-old Dorothea 'Dorothy' Waddingham married her lodger, former soldier Ronald Sullivan. As their family grew, she turned their house at 32 Devon Drive, Nottingham, into a nursing home in order to increase their income. Although she called herself 'Nurse' Waddingham, she was not a registered nurse, having failed to qualify, her only training having been as ward maid at an infirmary near Burton-on-Trent.

Impersonating a nurse was not the only crime thus far committed by the slightly-built Waddingham, who stood an inch under 5ft: during her marriage to Leech she had served prison sentences for fraud and theft.

Despite these convictions, in January 1935, on the recommendations of Nottingham Council, Mrs Louisa Baguley and her daughter, Ada, arrived at Devon Drive as their first patients. Both would prove to be demanding; the old lady, almost 90 years of age, needed constant medical assistance, while her daughter, at 50, was both disabled and obese and needed even more care.

Ada Baguley in her younger days.
(T.J. Leech Archive)

On 26 February, the only other resident died. The loss of income now caused Waddingham some consternation. She was already unhappy at the amount of care and time she had to devote to the mother and daughter in return for the income it drew. Nevertheless, she attended to the ladies to their apparent satisfaction – to the extent that on 6 May, Ada Baguley instructed her solicitor to change her will so that in the event of her death the proceeds of her insurance policies would pass to Nurse Waddingham and Ronald Sullivan. The will had been changed following an agreement from Dorothy to care for both women for the rest of their lives.

On 12 May, Louisa Baguley passed away. Her death caused no suspicion and she was buried a few days later. Waddingham continued to care for Ada over the following summer, but on September 11 Sullivan notified Dr H.H. Mansfield that Ada was in a coma. Mansfield called at the home and found that Ada was already dead. Mansfield had no cause to be suspicious and, after following consultation with Dorothy Waddingham, he filled out the death certificate stating that Ada died of cardio-vascular degeneration.

Apart from changing her will, Ada had given her permission to be cremated, and Waddingham arranged for it to take place on Friday 13 September. The date was to prove unlucky for Dorothy Waddingham. Before a cremation could be authorised, two doctors needed to sign a certificate, which could only be done after the family of the deceased was notified. It seemed Ada Baguley had put a clause into her will requesting not to notify her relatives.

The man in charge of cremations, known as the Crematorium Referee, was Dr Cyril Banks, also the Medical Officer for Health in Nottingham. Cremations were something of a rarity in 1936 and for one to be specified seemed unusual. Banks had suspicions about Waddingham's nursing home when he became aware there was no State Registered Nurse on the staff (as required by law). His suspicions were further raised when he heard of the note from Ada Baguley authorising cremation, and as a result he ordered a post-mortem.

Louisa Baguley's death certificate. (TNA: PRO)

No traces of anything connected to Ada's physical conditions that could have immediately caused death were found and, suspecting foul play, Banks ordered an analysis of the organs of the deceased. Considerable traces of morphine were found in her stomach, liver, kidneys and heart. In total, over three grains had been ingested. The police were notified and the body of Louisa was exhumed. Again, traces of morphine were found.

Armed with this knowledge, detectives questioned Waddingham and Sullivan. Both denied administering morphine, although Waddingham later changed her story to say she had done so on the advice of the womens' doctor. This was strenuously denied and both Sullivan and Waddingham were arrested and charged with murder.

'Nurse' Waddingham.
(Author's collection)

A coroner's jury found against them both and they were committed to stand trial before Mr Justice Goddard at Nottingham Assizes at the end of February 1936. Goddard decided there was insufficient evidence to proceed with charges against Sullivan and he was duly acquitted. The prosecution was handled by Norman Birkett, known mainly for his skills as a defence counsel. Birkett suggested the motive behind the murders was to gain the Baguleys' estate. On 27 February, after a two-week trial, 'Nurse' Waddingham was convicted on overwhelming evidence, with the jury surprisingly recommending mercy when returning a guilty verdict.

Thousands gathered in the streets outside the prison as Dorothy Waddingham spent her last hours in the condemned cell waiting for the fateful hour to arrive. Outside the prison walls wealthy abolitionist Mrs Violet Van der Elst organised a demonstration calling for the abolition of the death penalty. When word reached police headquarters of the size of the planned demonstration, they drafted in reinforcements from across the region, who assembled in an adjacent cinema until the demonstration approached the front gates. Officers then spilled out and blocked access to the gaol, while inside the would-be nurse, petty thief and murderer, walked bravely to the gallows.

25

THE COVENTRY OUTRAGE

Peter Barnes & James Richards, 7 February 1940

In January 1939, as the clouds of war were gathering in Europe, the high command of the IRA formulated the 'S' Plan, a bombing campaign to be launched on the British mainland. Its aims were primarily to focus attention on the request for the withdrawal of British troops from Ulster and a cessation of all claims by the British Government to interfere with the domestic policies of Ireland. An ultimatum given to then Prime Minister Neville Chamberlain expired on 16 January and, thenceforth, a campaign of terror was launched.

Initially, this was limited to attacks on 'soft targets', such as post office mailboxes and railway station cloakrooms and lavatories. As the campaign intensified, other explosions soon led to loss of life: a market worker was killed in a Manchester bombing and a Scottish doctor was fatally wounded following an explosion at London's King's Cross on 26 July.

The campaign reached its peak on Friday 25 August. That afternoon, Coventry's busy Broadgate was crowded with shoppers. At 2.32 p.m. there was an explosion outside paint merchants, John Astley & Sons. The blast shattered windows and left five people dead and another fifty injured. Those killed were 21-year-old bride-to-be Elsie Ansell, who was shopping in preparation for her forthcoming wedding; Gwilym Rowland, a 50-year-old Coventry Corporation worker; 81-year-old pensioner James Clay; John Corbett Arnott, a 15-year-old shop assistant; and a 33-year-old clerk, Rex Gentle.

The bomb had been placed in the pannier of a bicycle, which was left against the kerb. Detectives were able to recover the serial number from the remains of the bicycle and this led them to a branch of Halfords in Smithford Road. Shop assistants recalled the sale and this led police to James Richards, a 29-year-old plasterer's labourer from Westmead, Eire. Richards had been under Special Branch supervision since his arrival in Coventry several days before the explosion.

At the same time as Richards was being identified as a suspect in the 'Coventry Outrage', as it was dubbed in the press, detectives in London arrested five men on charges of the possession of explosives. One, 32-year-old Peter Barnes, had links with an address in Coventry and led detectives to 25 Clara Street, the home of Joseph and Mary Hewitt. Also living at the address were Brigid O'Hara, Mary's mother, and their lodger James Richards.

Detectives learned that Barnes had travelled to Clara Street four days before the bombing. Enquiries revealed that over the next few days Hewitt's mother-in-law, Brigid, had purchased a suitcase from Forey's store on Gosford Street, whilst Richards and another man had obtained the bicycle. On the day before the explosion, Richards had

Broadgate, Coventry, 25 August 1939. (TNA: PRO)

Emergency services on Broadgate. (TNA: PRO)

Clara Street, Coventry. (TNA: PRO)

made the bomb in the front room of the house, which, when searched, revealed further explosives hidden in a hole beneath the stairs. As a result of the investigation, the four occupants of Clara Street, along with Peter Barnes, were arrested and placed on trial for murder.

Armed detectives ringed Birmingham's Victoria Assize Courts and others patrolled the roof as their trial opened before Mr Justice Singleton on 11 December. All five were jointly convicted of the murder of Elsie Ansell, the only indictment being proceeded against at this stage. Elsie worked as a shop assistant at Cross Cheaping and had been due to marry two weeks after her untimely death. Her injuries had been so horrific that identification had only been possible by her engagement ring and fragments of clothing. The prosecution told the court that the bomb had been constructed by Richards, and possibly other untraced members of the IRA, in a room at Clara Street on the day before the explosion. The device was a combination of gelignite and potassium chlorate, which had been transported to the city by Peter Barnes. The timing device was an alarm clock, part of which was recovered from the house.

The court heard that the suspected target was probably a nearby power station, but mindful the bomb could go off at any time, the bombers had seemingly panicked whilst transporting it to the designated target and abandoned the bicycle on Broadgate. Although there was no direct evidence that Barnes had been involved in the planting of the bomb, there was enough evidence incriminating him in the bombing. A letter written by Barnes to a friend in Ireland outlined details of a proposed trip to the Midlands and three packets of potassium chlorate powder, the main component of the Coventry bomb, were found in Barnes' lodgings. Barnes' attempt to explain he had purchased them from a woman in Oxford Street, believing they were bath salts and other innocent toiletries, was dismissed as ludicrous.

Peter Barnes. (T.J. Leech Archive)

James Richards. (T.J. Leech Archive)

Bomb Murderers Die at 9 o'clock This Morning

LAST RITES GIVEN TO
DOOMED I.R.A. MEN

THE FOUR CARS IN THE NIGHT...

FOUR saloon cars slipped quietly into Winson Green Prison soon after darkness fell last night.

Passers-by noticed nothing unusual, but in them were Phillips, Cross, and the two Pierponts, who are hanging Barnes and Richards to-day.

The only hint was the quickness with which the prison doors opened to take them in.

The "Birmingham Gazette" understands that Barnes and Richards will be hanged at the same moment.

Two executioners will attend each man. The condemned men will see each other just before their deaths.

Last night guards of police and special constables maintained a constant patrol all round the gaol.

Factories, cinemas and public-houses were also especially watched.

Police informed the heads of a factory near the gaol that one of their watchmen was suspect.

But the factory heads were able to vouch for the youth. But it showed the care with which the police guarded against every possible "incident."

One Calm, One Breaks Down as Ring of Police Watch Birmingham Prison All Through Night

WHILE Peter Barnes and James Richards last night received last rites in the condemned cells at Winson Green Prison, Birmingham, from which they are due to go to their execution to-day, efforts were still being made in London to secure four more days for "conclusive proof" of their innocence of the Coventry bomb murders.

As the night wore on the last faint hopes of an eleventh-hour respite were fading. Both men had been told there was no hope. Richards, the "Birmingham Gazette" understands, was calm — as he said at the trial: "I am not afraid to die." But Barnes was in a state of partial collapse.

The men are to be hanged at nine a.m. to-day. They received the last rites of the Roman Catholic Church from Fr. ...

A news cutting detailing the imminent execution of IRA men Barnes and Richards. (Author's collection)

James Richards was a very different proposition. He readily admitted to being a member of the IRA and made little attempt to deny his involvement in the terror campaign. It soon became clear that the Hewitts and Mrs O'Hara had no links with any terrorist organisation and, although the suitcase used to transport the explosives had been purchased by Brigid O'Hara, she had purchased it unaware of its sinister purpose. As a result, all three were acquitted of the charges.

After a trial lasting four days, the jury took just thirty minutes to convict Barnes and Richards. The judge asked the accused if they had anything to say before sentence was passed. Barnes again claimed that he was innocent, but Richards took the opportunity to thank his defence team, claiming that his part in the explosions was part of a just cause. 'God Bless Ireland,' he shouted, before being ushered from the dock.

Despite protestations from members of the Irish government that the executions would merely turn the men into martyrs, Peter Barnes and James Richards were hanged side-by-side in the last double execution at Birmingham. As was the case at the trial, armed police ringed the gaol in order to prevent demonstrations and keep back curious sightseers while the executioner and his three assistants prepared the scaffold. Whilst inside, Richards was calm as he awaited the hangman, although it was reported that his fellow countryman spent his last hours highly distressed and in a partial state of collapse.

The remains of Barnes and Richards were later exhumed and reburied in Ireland, where a memorial stone was erected in their memory. (Crime Picture Archive)

26

INTEMPERATE HABITS

Eli Richards, 19 September 1941

Sixty-four-year-old hawker Jane Turner had been separated from her husband since the summer of 1939 on account of her drunkenness. She had soon found a position as a housekeeper with John Franklin on Farmer Street, Birmingham, but, as with her husband, Franklin found her intemperate habits too much to tolerate and he asked her to leave. Jane Turner left Farmer Street on Thursday, 27 March 1941, and was last seen by Franklin on the following morning when she returned to collect the rest of her belongings.

Later that day she made the acquaintance of 45-year-old Eli Richards, of Weoley Castle, a labourer at the ICI Metals factory. The landlord of The Bell public house on Bristol Street, Cotteridge, saw them enter at 9 p.m. and later that night Richards, who walked with the aid of a stick, was ejected. At twenty minutes to midnight, two Home Guard watchmen saw a couple they later recognised as Eli Richards and Jane Turner quarrelling in Bournville Lane. Richards was complaining they had been put off the tram at the wrong stop and were now lost. They asked for directions to Franklin Road and were seen walking off together. A short time later, screams were heard.

At daybreak on the Saturday morning the body of Jane Turner was found lying on the pavement on Franklin Road. She had been battered to death and in the road nearby were a walking stick, a blood-soaked handkerchief and a broken beer bottle. Investigations soon threw up the name of Eli Richards and he was picked up at his lodgings at 106 Castle Road that Sunday.

The body of Jane Turner lies on the pavement in Franklin Road. Eli Richards's walking stick is in the road. (TNA: PRO)

Richards had bloodstains on his clothes and scratches on his face. In his first statement he admitted that he had met Jane Turner in Bromsgrove Street. After drinking in The Bell, they had caught the number 71 tram to Franklin Road, where they had then quarrelled, but had soon made up their differences and Richards claimed that he had given Jane half a crown and walked away. He claimed that she was very much alive when he left her and he had never seen her again.

Richards denied that the walking stick found beside the body belonged to him. He claimed that he had lost this when he fell off a tram, which is where he received the scratches to his face. Travellers on the tram who had seen Richards and Mrs Turner alight from the bus disputed Richards' account that he had fallen. When further questioned, Richards claimed to have fallen whilst in Franklin Road and to have left his stick there.

Medical evidence found that Jane Turner had died as a result of multiple head injuries, probably caused by a bottle, and that the killer had made some attempt at a sexual assault. The blood on Richards' clothes, which he claimed was from a cut he had received, was found to be a different blood group, one identical to Mrs Turner's.

When the trial was heard before Mr Justice Stable at Birmingham Assizes on 22 July, Richards' defence counsel claimed that the prisoner was too drunk to remember events on the night Jane Turner died. They claimed he had merely argued, that the woman was known to have intemperate habits, and that she had provoked a very drunken Richards into attacking her, as a result of which he should be found guilty of manslaughter and not murder. The jury thought otherwise and returned a verdict of guilty as charged.

27

THE DESERTER

Arthur Peach, 30 January 1942

On Wednesday morning, 21 September 1941, two young girls, Kitty Lyons and Violet Richards, were strolling down a footpath known locally as the 'Cattle Arch' at Rushall, near Walsall, when a man in army uniform approached. No sooner had the girls walked past the soldier than a shot ring out. As Violet Richards slumped to the ground, Kitty Lyons screamed and fled up the path in terror, with the soldier in pursuit. Violet heard another shot rang out and saw Kitty fall to the ground. She then watched in horror as the soldier returned. With the butt of his gun, he battered Violet into unconsciousness. Kitty died from a single shot to the head, but Violet would eventually make a full recovery.

Witnesses told detectives they had seen a soldier in the area around the time of the murder and one man told police that he had seen the soldier standing near a ditch carrying a lady's handbag, while another saw a soldier throw something into a stream. A search in the shallow water recovered a Webley revolver, which matched the bullet removed from Kitty Lyon's head.

As the murder hunt began across the town, the killer was already in police custody. In the early hours of Thursday morning, 23-year-old army deserter Arthur Peach had been arrested by military police at his parents' home in Green Rock Lane, Bloxwich. Peach had enlisted into the South Staffordshire Regiment on 10 December 1939 and, after basic training at Lichfield, he was sent to a camp in Norfolk before the unit was moved to Tavistock, Devon. By September 1941, he had found the regime of army life not to his liking and deserted his unit, returning to his native Walsall.

When detectives investigating the murder heard about the soldier picked up for desertion, they interviewed Peach and, later that day, he was placed in an identity parade where witnesses who had been on the footpath at the time of the murder identified him. The gun recovered from the brook was identified by markings as a Webley stolen from a store in Devon, where Peach had been stationed prior to his absconding.

At his three-day trial before Mr Justice MacNaughton, which began at Stafford Assizes on 24 November, Peach admitted the theft of the gun, but he claimed that the revolver had no longer been in his possession at the time of the murder. He told the court that while he admitted to being on the footpath at the time of the murder, it was another deserter, a Scottish soldier he knew only as 'Jock', who had accidentally shot the girls whilst testing the revolver and that he had hurried to give assistance following the shooting. Finding the handbag, he had picked it up for safekeeping.

Above: *The 'Cattle Arch' at Rushall, near Walsall. (TNA: PRO)*

Right: *Notice of execution. (Author's collection)*

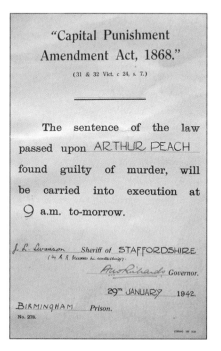

"Capital Punishment Amendment Act, 1868."

(31 & 32 Vict. c 24, s. 7.)

The sentence of the law passed upon ARTHUR PEACH found guilty of murder, will be carried into execution at 9 a.m. to-morrow.

J. L. Swanson Sheriff of STAFFORDSHIRE
(*by A. R. Stevens on instructions*)

Arthur Richards Governor.

29TH JANUARY 1942.

BIRMINGHAM Prison.

No. 278.

All the witnesses, including Violet Richards, testified to there being only one soldier on the footpath and Peach's version of events was deemed to be untrue. The prosecution claimed that Peach, acting alone, had intended to steal from the young ladies and that during the robbery he had resorted to murder.

Peach protested his innocence and claimed Scotland Yard detectives had assaulted him during his interrogation. The court heard that Peach had come from a broken home and that he had been involved in petty crime most of his life, but a troubled upbringing was no excuse for murder and Peach was found to be guilty as charged.

28

TO BE TOGETHER IN THE NEXT LIFE

Harold Oswald Merry, 10 September 1942

In the summer of 1941, Harold Merry, a 40-year-old married man with five children, met 27-year-old Joyce Dixon when she started work as a typist at Austin Aero Factory in Birmingham, where he was employed as an inspector. Merry initially told her he was a single man, but as their courtship progressed he confided in her that he was actually married, but was separated from his wife. This was untrue; Merry was still living with his wife, to all intents and purposes as a happily married couple.

Unaware her lover still lived with his wife and family, Joyce sent Merry a love letter while both were on holiday from work that September. Merry's wife opened the letter and, reading the contents, she immediately threw him out. Failing to convince her to take him back, Merry packed his bags and went to live with his sister in Redditch.

Merry and Joyce continued their courting and, on 20 March 1942, Merry asked Joyce's parents for permission to marry her. After being granted consent, they went to stay in London for a few days, returning on Friday 27 March. Joyce's parents were unaware their daughter's boyfriend was a married man with a young family and when they discovered this they told them they would not give their blessing to the relationship and that Merry was no longer welcome at their house.

Their protection of their daughter's interests was understandable. Although Joyce was now in her late twenties, during her teens she had suffered from a number of mental health problems and had been receiving medical attention up until September 1938. Apparently recovered, she had been able to find work as a typist, but her parents were aware that these health problems could return if she was to become shocked and upset.

On the following Sunday, 29 March, Joyce left her home in the afternoon, saying she was meeting Merry. When she failed to return home that night a search was launched and one of her brothers, Victor, called to see Merry. Merry was upstairs in his room when the caller knocked at the door and, when he saw who it was, he made an attempt to strangle himself with a flex from the electric light. Victor Dixon pulled the flex from Merry's neck and asked where his sister was.

'You have murdered her, haven't you?' Dixon shouted.

'That's right, she's in the brook,' Merry told him.

As Merry was taken into custody, officers went to a pool at nearby Turves Green, close to Joyce's family home at Northfield, where they found her body. Medical

102

evidence would show that Joyce had been strangled to the point of unconsciousness before being placed into the water, although the cause of death was drowning. Merry made a full confession, but then, on Wednesday 2 April, he changed his mind and said he wished to withdraw that plea.

At his trial before Mr Justice Croom-Johnson at Warwickshire Assizes, held in Birmingham on 17 July, Merry's defence was that he had killed Joyce as part of a suicide pact and that his attempt to hang himself from a light flex in his room was in order to keep his side of the bargain. He had committed the murder, he told the court, so that they could be together in the next life.

Merry had showed detectives a hand-written note, which both he and Joyce had signed. He claimed that they had gone to the field, where he had killed Joyce before attempting to strangle himself with a tie. When this failed, he tried to drown himself, but the water was not deep enough, so he reluctantly returned home.

PART B.
CORONER'S ORDER FOR BURIAL.
Form prescribed by Rules made by the Lord Chancellor under the Coroners (Amendment) Act, 1926.

I, the undersigned, Coroner for the...... **City** ....

of..... **Birmingham,** ....do hereby authorise the burial

of the body of...... **Harold Oswald Merry,** ....

aged about..**41 years,** ....late of..**205, Hewell Road,**
Redditch, Worcestershire,

whose death was reported to me on.. **10th September 1942**

and whose body has been viewed by me*(and by the inquest jury).

Witness my hand this.... **10th** ....day of **September** 19 42 .

*Strike out
if inapplicable. .... _Daukberson_ - _Deput_ Coroner.

IMPORTANT.—This certificate must be preserved with care and delivered intact (*i.e.*, without detaching Part C) to the person effecting the disposal of the body, as to whom SEE BACK. The burial may be stopped if this certificate is not so delivered.

If it is intended to remove the body out of England and Wales, notice must be given to the Coroner in advance of the removal. A form for giving notice may be obtained from the Coroner.

. This Certificate will authorise the burial in a burial ground of the remains of a stillborn child.

This certificate is of no use for the purpose of cremation.

The Coroner is requested to fill in spaces 1 and 2 of Part C of this form (see penultimate paragraph on cover).

Form 101.

The Coroner's Order for the burial of executed prisoner Harold Merry. (Author's collection)

The judge directed the jury it was for them to decide if this was a case of murder or manslaughter. Although the motive for the crime was vague, the prosecution claimed it had been committed by a man who had then tried to make it appear as if it was part of a suicide pact, when there was nothing to suggest that Merry's attempts to take his own life were genuine.

29

BENEATH THE RUBBLE

William Quayle, 3 August 1943

Eight-year-old Vera Clarke had not been seen since she left Piggott Street School and failed to return to her nearby home on Essington Street, Birmingham, on the afternoon of Friday, 5 May 1943. After a fruitless search, the police were called.

In the meantime, her worried family conducted their own enquiries and spoke to school friends of Vera, who gave them some interesting information. Vera had left school at 4.30 p.m., parting from her friends outside the school gates. Fifteen minutes later, she was seen by 10-year-old William Abbotts standing on the doorstep of 132a Bath Row. Vera was holding her skipping rope and had been talking to the man who lived there. William saw the man give Vera a piece of paper and watched as she headed off down the street.

Thirteen-year-old Dorothy Binnion had also heard about Vera's disappearance and when she bumped into schoolteacher Reginald London on the following morning, she told him she had also seen Vera outside the house on Bath Row and that the front door was open. Mr London and Dorothy went round to see Vera's parents, Charles and Ada Clarke, and agreed to accompany them to Bath Row to follow up the lead.

Arriving outside, Ada Clarke rapped on the door and, as it slowly opened, she addressed the occupant.

'I'm sorry to bother you, but I'm asking after my daughter. She's missing.'

'Well why ask me?' the occupent, William Quayle, replied indignantly as he viewed the group before him. Mr London then addressed him. 'She was seen on the doorstep of this house. Do you know anything about her? These are her parents and this girl saw her here last night after school.'

'I don't know your daughter. Sorry,' Quayle said, making to close the door.

'But you sent her on an errand,' Mr London insisted.

Quayle continued with his denial and claimed that his door had not been opened at all since the following afternoon, despite what Dorothy had told them.

They asked if they could come inside and see for themselves and Quayle invited them in. They checked that the rooms were empty and then asked about the cellar door. Quayle told them the cellar wasn't used, that it was kept locked from the inside and the only entrance was via a rusty metal grate in the back yard. The group followed Quayle outside, where he made a vain attempt to lift the grate, explaining to them that it was very heavy and hadn't been opened for quite some time. Satisfied that Vera was not in the house, they departed, with Mr London telling Quayle they were going to the police and asking if he would be home later if officers wanted to speak to him.

Quayle said he would be, adding, 'I shall wait all day for them. I've nothing to be afraid of.'

At the police station they reported what Quayle had told them and Sergeant Cyril Smith made his way to Bath Row in the company of Ada Clarke. There was no reply to his knocking. Ada showed the officer the cellar grate and, although Quayle had made a great play of it being stuck fast and heavy, the sergeant was able to lift it easily and ease himself into the cellar. Within minutes he emerged holding a child's coat. Ada burst into tears as she recognised it as belonging to her missing daughter. A further search also found her skipping rope inside the house.

As the search for William Quayle intensified, it was learned that he had lived in the house on Bath Row since May of the previous year, with his wife and family, but for the last two weeks he had lived alone after they had walked out on him following a blazing row. He had a long police record, had served a number of prison sentences for various crimes, and was known to resort to violence when drunk.

Later that afternoon, Quayle was recognised by a police officer as he walked along Broad Street.

'What are you talking about? I don't know anything about any missing girl,' he blustered when told he was wanted for questioning. Despite his denials, Quayle was seized by the arm and escorted into custody, where detectives questioned him.

Quayle denied any knowledge of Vera's whereabouts. He claimed he was asleep in a chair that afternoon and that his door had not been opened at 5 p.m. despite what the children had told them. He said he had eaten something for tea and had left for work at 5.40 p.m. He said that he had arrived at work, but after telling his bosses that he was feeling unwell as a result of having some teeth removed, he was allowed to go home and left within the hour. Quayle said that instead of going home he had gone to a number of public houses, leaving at closing time and sleeping until that morning and the visit from Vera's parents and schoolteacher. He said he had no idea how Vera's coat could have been found in his cellar and her skipping rope down the side of his sofa.

Quayle was detained in the cells while further enquiries were made and at 9.30 p.m. that night Detective Inspector Bill Anderson had Quayle brought back to the interview room. This time the interview was lead by Superintendent Richardson.

No sooner had Quayle taken his seat than he blurted out, 'You want to find her ... I'll take you to her.'

At this, pathologist Professor James Webster was summoned and a short time later, in the company of the detectives and the suspect, he arrived at a bombed-out house on Spring Vale in nearby Edgbaston. As they reached No. 12, Quayle pointed to the doorway.

'There,' he said, pointing to a pile of rubble inside the back door. Webster walked over and lifted a number of bricks as the detectives held torches to light up the scene. Vera Clarke lay beneath the debris; she was naked apart from a pair of socks and one shoe.

The bombed house on Spring Vale, where Vera Clarke's body was discovered. (TNA: PRO)

Left: *Vera Clarke. (Author's collection)*

Below: *A coroner's jury viewed the body of William Quayle after execution. (Author's collection)*

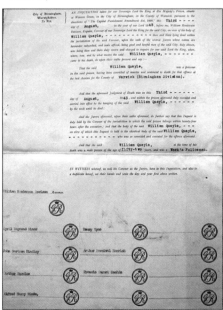

As the body was removed to the mortuary for the post-mortem, Quayle was returned to the station, where he made a further statement and admitted that he had indeed sent Vera on an errand. She had gone to fetch him some potatoes from a greengrocer and when she returned to the house Quayle said he had just snapped, rushed at her and had strangled her. He said he had left the body lying on the rug and gone to work, where, after making a telephone call to his manager, he had clocked off and spent the night drinking. He had woken in the early hours, loaded her body onto a cart and then wheeled it to Spring Vale, where he concealed it in the rubble.

Although he appeared eager to co-operate with detectives, Quayle was still not telling the whole truth. The post-mortem found that Vera had been brutally raped before she had been strangled. Quayle, while readily admitting the murder, denied the sexual assault.

At his trial before Mr Justice Wrottesley at Birmingham Assizes on 13 July, Quayle said that he had been drinking heavily since his wife had left him and when Vera returned from running an errand he had a 'brain storm'. His defence counsel claimed there was no 'malice aforethought' and tried for a verdict of manslaughter, also claiming that Quayle was insane. The court heard that while on remand pending trial, Quayle had become ill from hypostatic pneumonia, and X-rays found that he had ingested a number of items including an opened safety pin, presumably in order to attempt to cheat the hangman.

The rational way in which Quayle had made his confession to the police was picked up by the prosecution to suggest there was no sign of insanity. The jury were clearly unsympathetic to Quayle and quickly returned a verdict of guilty of murder. They made no recommendation for mercy, there was no appeal, and the brutal child-killer kept his 9 o'clock appointment with the hangman on a warm, summer morning.

30

THE HOLLY BUSH STRANGLER

James Farrell, 29 March 1949

On Sunday afternoon, 21 November 1948, 14-year-old Joan Mary Marney visited the Perry Barr Odeon cinema with two school friends. The Sunday matinee show was always popular and by the time the girls were shown to the stalls they were unable to find three seats together. There were, however, two seats on the front row and an empty pair directly behind them and, while her two friends sat together at the front, Joan took one of those behind. No sooner had she taken her seat than a young, fair-haired soldier, wearing khaki battle-dress, took his place in the empty seat, smiling at Joan as he did so.

As they waited for the film to commence, he began chatting to her and, when the programme finished, the soldier, who gave his name as Jim, continued talking with Joan. As they left the cinema, he discovered she lived at Kingstanding and, as he was going that way, he asked if he could escort her home. Her friends giggled as Joan accepted his offer and they walked off while Joan and the soldier headed towards the bus stop. It was a little after 6.30 p.m.

An hour later, when they had reached Kingstanding, Joan agreed to the soldier's request to go for a walk on condition that he would see her home before 9.30 p.m. The soldier agreed and they set off in the direction of Sutton Park. It was to be a fateful mistake. When Joan failed to return home at her usual time that evening her worried parents contacted her friends, who told them about the young soldier she had gone off with after leaving the cinema. When there was still no sign of her by midnight, they called the police, who listed her as missing and began a search.

On the following morning, nurse Bertram Rennie, making his way to work through a fog-covered Sutton Park, noticed a woman's handbag lying close to the Banners Gate entrance. As he bent down to pick up the handbag, he discovered the body of Joan Marney lying beneath a holly bush. Rennie checked for any signs of life and, finding she was dead, hurried to notify the police.

A post-mortem carried out by Professor James Webster found that Joan had been strangled and that the killer had forced part of her raincoat into her mouth, presumably to stifle her screams. She had not been raped, although it seemed the killer had attempted

The entrance to Sutton Park. (TNA: PRO)

It was the handbag lying on the ground that led to Joan Marney's body being discovered lying in holly bushes in Sutton Park. (TNA: PRO)

A close-up of the body of Joan Marney. (TNA: PRO)

to sexually assault her. A murder enquiry was launched and detectives interviewed Joan's school friends, who furnished them with a detailed description of the fair-haired young soldier.

Meanwhile, a few miles away, a young man walked into Steelhouse Lane police station. He gave his name as 18-year-old James Farrell and claimed he had absconded from the Royal Army Service Corps and wished to give himself up as a deserter. The desk sergeant was already aware of the murder enquiry in Sutton Coldfield, with information relating to a wanted soldier, and asked him to wait while he spoke to detectives in Birmingham.

Detective Inspector Thomas Medley, leading the enquiry, hurried to Sutton Coldfield. Medley claimed later that he knew at once that he was face-to-face with a killer. Farrell was questioned about the murder and immediately launched into a full confession. He said that he had met Joan at the cinema, that they got talking and she had told him that she was seventeen and a half years old. Joan was a healthy, well-built young girl who did look older than her years and Farrell had no reason to doubt her.

He invited her to go for a walk in Sutton Park and she agreed. Once in the park Farrell attempted to kiss her, but when his advances became more than just kissing, Joan protested and asked to go home. Farrell then led her towards the holly bushes and pushed her onto the ground. She had began to cry and, as he pulled at her clothes, she told him her real age and said if he did not stop she would report him to the police. Farrell said that he then put his hands around her neck while he continued to kiss her and then, as she struggled, he squeezed his hands tighter, pushing part of her raincoat into her mouth until she ceased to resist.

At his trial before Mr Justice Lynskey at Warwick Assizes on 10 March, Farrell's defence was that he was insane. On the day before the murder, his father had found him semi-conscious in front of the gas stove at their home. In what appeared to be an attempt at suicide, the gas tap was turned on fully, but the gas had run out. The defence also claimed insanity was hereditary and that Farrell's mother had been an inmate in Lodge Road Asylum for the past three and a half years.

Farrell sat with his hands resting on his chin throughout the trial and it was reported that he seemed to be 'chillingly indifferent' to the fate of the young schoolgirl. The prosecution refuted the defence's claims and stated that it was a brutal murder, made during the course of a sexual assault, and that the young girl had been killed because she had threatened to report him for that assault. They claimed there was nothing to suggest Farrell was insane and that, despite his youth, he was fully aware of his actions and the consequences of these actions, and that by attempting to be arrested for desertion he had hoped to be locked up away from the police investigations and so evade justice. These actions also suggested that he knew what he had done was wrong and were not the actions of someone suffering from insanity. The jury of eleven men and one woman needed just a short time to return a guilty verdict. Farrell turned nineteen just a few days before he was led to the gallows and was one of the youngest men to be executed in the twentieth century.

Hangman Syd Dernley was present at the execution as a witness to gain experience before being entrusted with the responsibilities of a *bona fide* assistant. He recalled that at the stroke of 8 a.m. he was ushered into the execution chamber while Albert Pierrepoint

ACCUSED OF B'HAM GIRL'S MURDER

YOUNG SOLDIER'S BRIEF COURT APPEARANCE

COUPLE'S MEETING IN CINEMA DESCRIBED

Wearing a brown sports jacket and grey flannel trousers, an 18-year-old soldier made a five-minute appearance at Sutton Coldfield Magistrates' Court

A recent picture of Joan Marney (right) with her mother.

The victim and her mother as they were pictured in the local press. (TNA: PRO)

and his assistant Harry Kirk entered the condemned cell. Dernley said that, as he entered the chamber, he noticed that a pair of yellow folding doors had been thrown open, and within seconds Pierrepoint appeared through these doors, followed by the prisoner with the most terrified eyes he had ever seen.

Pierrepoint, wearing a smart blue lounge suit and with what appeared to be a foppishly-worn white handkerchief in his breast pocket, led the youth onto the trapdoors, stopped, turned around and stretched out his arms, halting the prisoner on the chalk mark he had made to position his feet over.

Sutton Park Murder Charge

YOUNG SOLDIER'S ALLEGED STORY OF STRUGGLE IN WOOD

"The prosecution are submitting that this young man deliberately and cruelly strangled this 14-year-old schoolgirl," said Mr. Paul Sandlands, K.C., prosecuting for the Crown when the trial opened at Warwick Assizes to-day of an 18-year-old Birmingham soldier, James Farrell, of 4, Bevis Grove, Dormington Road, Kingstanding, who pleaded not guilty to a charge of murdering Joan Mary Marney, of 75, Sidcup Road, Kingstanding, on the night of November 21, in Sutton Park.

In his evidence, Nathaniel Farrell, father of the accused, described how on the day before the park tragedy he found his son semi-conscious lying in front of the gas-stove at their home. The gas tap was on, but the supply had run out.

The trial was before Mr. Justice Lynskey, and Farrell was represented by Mr. R. C. Vaughan, K.C. and Mr. Geoffrey Lane

cruelly strangled by a man's hands.

On November 22 Farrell went to Steelhouse Lane police station to give himself up as an absentee, and was recognised as answering the description of a man wanted in connection with the girl's death.

Eventually he said: "Yes, it was me. I took her to the park and then strangled her. He made

Farrell's crime made headlines in the local papers. (TNA: PRO)

The 'handkerchief' was in fact the white hood used to cover the prisoner's head and, once Farrell was in position, Pierrepoint whipped it from his pocket, placed it over his head and then deftly placed the noose, while Kirk swooped down and secured his ankles. Pierrepoint then reached to his left and as Kirk leapt off the trap he pushed the lever and Farrell plunged to his death. The entire execution had taken just eight seconds.

31

SUICIDE PACT

Piotr Maksimowski, 29 March 1950

In the early hours of 31 December 1949, a man approached a police station at Beaconsfield, Buckinghamshire, and began hammering on the door. The officer in charge then found himself confronted by a distraught, dishevelled and blood-soaked man, who, showing them his wrists, cut and bleeding, mumbled in broken English, 'I did it with razor. I do same to a girl in the woods ...'

Officers went to where the man directed them and discovered the body of a woman, covered in a blanket with both her wrists cut. The man gave his name as 33-year-old Piotr Maksimowski and claimed he was a Polish refugee who had settled in England at the end of the war and lived in a hostel on a camp at Great Bower Wood, near Beaconsfield, Buckinghamshire. He said the dead woman was his 30-year-old girlfriend, Dilys Campbell.

The body of Dilys Campbell as discovered by police. (TNA: PRO)

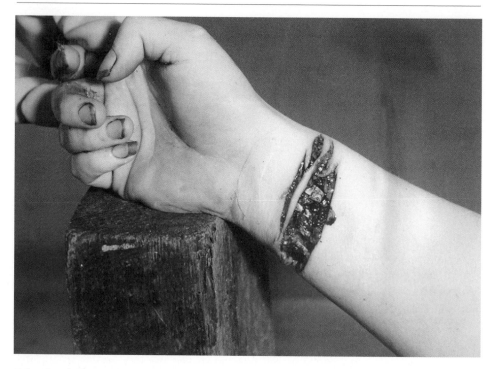

Dilys Campbell's wounds were so deep it was clear she had not taken her own life. (TNA: PRO)

Maksimowski said he had been courting Dilys for several months, and that she had initially told him she had been widowed. Once the relationship developed into something heavier, she had then confessed to him that not only was her husband very much alive but that they even still lived together, along with their two children, in Slough. Both knew that the relationship was wrong, but, although they tried to end it, they could not stop seeing each other.

Maksimowski said that they had then agreed on a suicide pact because she could not face living a lie, and he could not stand to know she still lived with her husband. On the previous evening they had been out for drinks in Windsor and Maksimowski told Dilys he was going home alone. She said she wanted to go with him and they both took a taxi to the camp and then went for a walk together in Great Bower Wood.

Here, he said, at her insistence, they decided to go ahead with their pact. After helping her to cut her throat and wrists, Maksimowski claimed that he had lost his nerve and had called the police in the hope she could get medical attention.

Questioned by detectives, the Pole stuck to his story, even though a post-mortem had found that her wounds were deep – the ones on her wrists were down to the bone, yet once the blood was wiped off Maksimowski's wounds, there was little more that a scratch. He also had trouble accounting for the scratches on his face, which detectives believed were signs of a struggle. Finally he cracked and admitted that Dilys had tried to change her mind at the last moment, but he had helped her go through with the pact and, after cutting her throat and wrists, he had covered her with the blanket and then cut himself. Convinced that they were not dealing with a case of suicide, police placed Maksimowski under arrest and charged him with wilful murder.

At his trial before Mr Justice Croom-Johnson at Warwick Assizes in March, Maksimowski pleaded not guilty on the grounds of insanity. It was shown that Maksimowski's claim to have gone straight for help after cutting Dilys's wrists was untrue and that Dilys Campbell had been dead for at least four hours when a doctor reached the scene.

Once sentence of death had been passed on him, Maksimowski, speaking through an interpreter, asked if he could be shot instead of being hanged. The judge told him he had no power to deal with the matter as it had passed out of his hands. There was no appeal, but a few days before he went to the gallows the Pole made a failed attempt to commit suicide by breaking a window in his cell and trying to cut his wrists on the broken glass.

Translation from Polish

To:- Mr. Leslie Pocock, Solicitor,
        Hutton - Pocock,
            6, Burkes Parade,
                Beaconsfield, Bucks.

From:- P. Maksimowski,
            No. 3858 H.M. Prison, Birmingham.

9th March, 1950.

Dear Mr Solicitor,

I received your letter for which I thank you, and I thank you for help in my case.

I apologize for having caused you, Mr Solicitor, further trouble, I agreed with the verdict, although not all the prosecutor and the Chief Judge said was true.

I would ask you to send me all my letters and generally all my papers (copy books). I want to destroy part, part I want to send away and I want to copy certain parts, which were roughly written. My belongings, such as linen and suits, I should like to be sent to my Mother in Poland. I should like everything to be sent to the dry cleaners, the trousers are blood stained. This is to be paid for with my money. The address is:- Jadwiga Maksimowska, Swierczewski Street 30, Brzeg on/Oder, Lower Silesia, Poland. (Ul Swierczewskiego 30, Brzeg N/Odre, Dolny Slask).

I personally need nothing - all I am short of are Polish Books, but that is of no importance.

My belongings are at the Police Station at Beaconsfield; a suitcase containing papers is there too.

If I have any further request to make, I will appeal to you again, Mr Solicitor.

Once again I thank you very much for all your trouble, and I thank the Welfare Officer.

(signed)   P. Maksimowski

Maksimowski's letter to his solicitor following conviction. (TNA: PRO)

Left: *Albert Pierrepoint (left) was assisted by Syd Dernley (right) on several executions at Birmingham, including Maksimowski's. (Crime Picture Archive)*

Below: *Official prison details issued on the day of Maksimowski's execution. (Author's collection)*

All communications should be
addressed to "The Governor"
and not to any official by name.

H. M. PRISON,

Birmingham
March 29 th. 50.

Piotr   Macksimowski   Regd.   No. 3858.

Notice of execution posted outside the main gates at 9-30 am. 28 3 1950
by Engr Orme.
Above notice taken down and cards Nos.279 and 280 posted in its place by
C. O. Doney on 29 3 1950.
The execution was carried out by Executioner A. Pierpoint and assistant
Mr. Dernley at 9-0 am. on 29 3 1950.
The body was examined after execution by the Medical Officers Dr. Humphrey
and Dr. Wray. who pronounced life extinct at 9-11 am.
The body was taken down at 10-0 am. by Engrs Sanders, Orme, and Offrs, Bowen
and Burgess and laid in the coffin ready for the Coroners inquest in the
viewing room.
The Coroner and Jury visited the body at 10-25 am. afterwards signing the
Inquisition Certificate.
The above certificate was posted outside the gate at 11-15 am. by Engr.
Sanders.
Weight of prisoner 168 lbs. height 5 ft. 8 ins. Drop 5 ft. 7½ ins.
Grave Diggers G. Pallet, and A. Guest   from Handsworth Cemetary Tel
                                                  N.O.R.0096
Body removed to Burial ground at 11-45 am to await burial.
Burial at 12-0 noon , service by Father Boland, who also officiated at the
execution, C.O. Wood, Engrs Sanders and Orme and Offrs Bowen and Burgess,
the latter two Offrs filling in the grave which was completed at 1-15 pm.
Charcoal used 56 lbs after 1 ft, of earth had been put over the coffin.
Depth of grave 7 ft.6 ins.No. 19,4ft. from tower and 2 ft. from boundary wall
Execution boxes returned to Stewards Stores, and execution rooms securely
locked, Keys returned to the Governer.

32

THE UNWANTED BURDEN OF RESPONSIBILITY

William Arthur Watkins, 3 April 1951

Hangman Albert Pierrepoint was taken aback as he spied the prisoner he was to hang on the following morning. With his eye pressed tight against the small Judas hole in the prison door he peered into the cell, studied the prisoner briefly, and then stared again at the details he had been handed containing the details of the condemned man. According to the piece of paper the man's age was given as 49 years old, but as Pierrepoint observed the sad, grey-haired man silently for several minutes he thought he seemed much, much older, closer to 70, he later noted.

The prisoner was William Arthur 'Bill' Watkins, a 49-year-old enameller who lived at 6 back 79 Clifton Road, Balsall Heath, Birmingham. Watkins was a married man, but had been associating for five years with a young woman named Florence 'Maisie' White. They already had a three-year-old child together when Maisie discovered she was pregnant again.

She duly gave birth to a healthy baby boy and in the early hours of Sunday 21 January 1951, Watkins took the baby into the bathroom and said he was going to give the baby a bath. A short time later Watkins told Maisie that while bathing the child it has slipped into the water and drowned. Although both claimed to be shocked by the accident, they did not report it to the police.

An early photograph of William Watkins.
(T.J. Leech Archive)

In due course the matter did come to the attention of the police. They visited Clifton Road and found the child's body, inside a pillowcase. Watkins, who was profoundly deaf, was unable to give satisfactory answers to why he had failed to notify anyone of the child's death, and moreover why the body was concealed in the pillowcase.

A post-mortem suggested that the baby had already been placed in the pillowcase before it was immersed in the bathtub, which dispelled the claim it had drowned accidentally. Police officers also learned that Watkins had lied to friends and neighbours by claiming that Maisie had been attended to by a doctor and midwife, both during her confinement and following the birth.

The two-day trial took place at Birmingham Assizes before Mr Justice Finnemore in March. Watkins' deafness meant that a warder sat next to him in the dock and translated the evidence to him. The prosecution claimed that Watkins had killed the child to be rid of the unwanted burden of responsibility, while the accused maintained that the child's death was an accident and that the baby had slipped under the water. The jury deliberated for two and a half hours before finding Watkins guilty of murder and he was returned to Winson Green to await execution.

He had a tearful last meeting with his estranged wife and children shortly before his execution and his son was among those outside the prison gates when the notices were posted on Tuesday 3 April to show that Pierrepoint had gone about his task with the usual efficiency.

33

THE MAN NEXT DOOR

Horace Carter, 1 January 1952

'I wish I could put the clock back forty-eight hours, but it's no good talking now, it is too late. I wonder how I shall get on for insurance if I get my neck stretched?'
Statement made by Horace Carter following his arrest in August 1951.

It was just before 6 p.m. on Wednesday, 1 August 1951, when 11-year-old Sheila Ethel Attwood left her home on Caversham Road, Kingstanding, which, at the time, was the largest municipal housing estate in the city. Sheila was one of a family of nine and, telling her mother she was going to play with school friends, as she did most evenings, she mounted her bicycle and pedalled away.

She was last seen heading towards a gully 200 yards from her home. When she failed to return home that night, her worried parents alerted neighbours and a frantic search took place. As darkness fell, the police were notified and the search continued until the following morning, when a neighbour, looking over railings at the bottom of her garden, discovered a young girl's body behind a hedge separating Caversham Road from a public works yard owned by Birmingham Corporation. She was partly concealed beneath some bushes with just her legs protruding. The neighbour's cries brought Sheila's mother rushing from the house, where her worse fears were confirmed.

With the body quickly identified as that of the missing girl, a police doctor certified Sheila was dead at the scene and a post-mortem found that cause of death was strangulation following attempted suffocation; string had been wrapped around her neck and there were finger marks where the killer had used his hands to strangle the young girl. She had also been raped.

The body had been found adjacent to house No. 32 and a routine questioning of

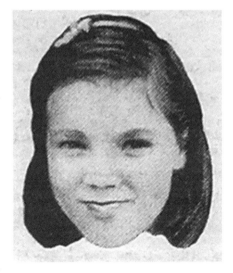

Sheila Attwood. (Author's collection)

Mrs Attwood is distraught at the discovery of her daughter's body. (Author's collection)

all the neighbours soon lead police to 30-year-old labourer Horace Carter, who lived at No. 34. Carter was quick to deny any involvement in the murder: 'I know nothing about her death. My conscience is clear,' he told detectives. Despite his denials, Carter's demeanour aroused suspicions in the officers and he was asked to accompany them to the station for further questioning.

As they approached Kingstanding police station Carter suddenly became all emotional and blurted out, 'I never really intended to hurt the girl ...' He instructed detectives to take him back to his house, where he said he would explain what had happened and how he had carried out the attack.

Carter said he had returned home from work around 6 p.m. when he saw Sheila pushing her bicycle, which he noticed had a flat tyre. He offered to repair the puncture and as he was well known to the young girl she accepted the offer and entered the house. Carter's family were on holiday at the time and the only person staying there was his brother-in-law, who was still at work. He offered Sheila some sweets while he repaired the bicycle and when he had completed it he made some pretext to invite her upstairs, without any evil intentions he told officers, and she had followed him. There, he said, he pushed her down onto the bed and raped her. He then panicked that she would report what he had done and, fearful of the consequences, he pushed a pillow over her face and tried to smother her.

Horace Carter, the man next door. (Author's collection)

LIST OF PREVIOUS CONVICTIONS

Name ....Horace..CARTER..
28.3.1921. Birmingham.   (See over for Notes)

General Reg. No. (in case of convicts) ....C..R..O..No..31827/38.

Sentence (1)	Court and Place (2)	Date (3)			Offence (4)	Name in full in which convicted (5)
B.O.£5 12mths.	J.C.B'ham.	1	12	38	Stg. cycle.	
Dis.P.O.A.	–do–	15	3	39	Stg. £5.	
B.O.12mths.	Coventry.	18	3	39	Stg. cycle.	
3yrs. P.S.	Ass. B'ham.	3	12	46	Robbery whilst armed with offensive weapon.; Robbery with violence.	
	2 Summaries:Defraud Railway;Fail conf. T/sign cycle.					

Horace Carter's criminal record. (Author's collection)

'She struggled a bit and to finish her more quickly I put my fingers around her throat. After that she ceased struggling,' Carter told officers, adding,

She was still breathing so I decided to use some string. I found some in the drawer and tied it around her throat. Either I was weak and didn't like doing it, or she was tougher than I thought. She was still breathing so I went and got some cloth and my handkerchief and tied it around her mouth and nostrils and turned her face down on the bed.

Carter said he then left her in the praying position and waited 'in patience' for darkness before he took some ladders from the shed and used them to lift her lifeless body over the back fence and dump her in the yard. On the following day he made a further statement, adding that he wished he could put the clock back.

Horace Carter stood trial before Mr Justice Cassels on 12 December at Birmingham Assizes. His counsel chose the only option open to them: Carter was guilty, but insane. They claimed that Carter possessed a psychopathic personality, indifferent to his own fate, or the death of others. The court heard how Carter had attempted suicide by shooting himself in the stomach and that he owned a number of books detailing infamous murders.

A number of doctors testified for both the prosecution and the defence, but the most damning testimony came from Dr J.J. O'Reilly, Medical Superintendent at Winson Green Gaol, who told the court that he believed Carter had a 'mental kink', but that at

BIRMINGHAM MURDERER PAYS PENALTY

Crowds read the notice of execution outside the prison gates on New Year's Day, 1952. (Crime Picture Archive)

the time he committed the crime he was legally sane. Following the judge's summing up, the jury, which included three women, needed just fifteen minutes to find Carter guilty of murder.

Carter's execution was fixed for Tuesday, 1 January 1952, and as a result hangmen Albert Pierrepoint and Syd Dernley spent New Year's Eve in their quarters at the prison, as revellers celebrated outside the prison walls. Dernley later recorded that of the score of killers he helped execute, none had aroused the revulsion of prison staff quite as much as Horace Carter.

34

PRIME SUSPECT

Leslie Terrence Green, 23 December 1952

Early on Wednesday evening, 16 July 1952, Cuthbert Fredrick Wiltshaw finished his game of bridge and made his way home. Wiltshaw, a wealthy company director who ran a successful pottery business, had lived alone with his 62-year-old wife Alice at 'Estoril', a fourteen-roomed mansion at Barlaston, Staffordshire, since their four daughters had all left home and married. Wiltshaw's daily routine was such that, after leaving work, he would stop off for a drink and a game of bridge with friends before returning home in time for tea.

As he entered through the back kitchen door, Wiltshaw could tell at once that something was amiss. On the kitchen floor lay a saucepan with a broken handle in a pool of water and raw vegetables. In the adjacent hallway he recoiled at the dreadful sight that greeted him. Alice Wiltshaw lay in a pool of blood, her skull staved in, her nose flattened and her jaw shattered. Her face and upper body was a mass of cuts and bruises and beside the body were the remains of a broken vase and a heavy brass poker. A pathologist later recorded that the wounds had completely drained the body of blood.

Alice Wiltshaw. (Author's collection)

Wiltshaw hurried from the house and summoned a neighbour, Dr Harold Browne, who telephoned for the police. Browne needed only a cursory glance to see that Alice Wiltshaw was dead and, as they waited for detectives to arrive, Browne lead Wiltshaw into the garden where they noticed a pair of cream leather gloves close to some bushes at the end of the garden.

The local police immediately asked for the assistance of Scotland Yard and quick to the scene were Detective Superintendent Reginald Spooner and his sergeant, Ernest Millen. As in every case of murder, detectives had to eliminate all possible suspects, including immediate family, and once Wiltshaw was able to satisfy the detectives of his innocence, the murder enquiry began.

It seemed clear that the motive was robbery; jewellery, including rings and a brooch, along with a wallet and a purse had been taken from the house. A purple leather case containing jewellery worth over £3,000 was missing and the killer had wrenched two rings from the dead woman's fingers, a baguette ring and an eternity ring. One unusual item noted as missing was an old RAF greatcoat that hung in the kitchen. Detectives also discovered distinctive, patterned footprints on the kitchen floor.

A check on employees at the house, both past and present, eliminated many people from enquiries, with one exception: former chauffeur-cum-gardener Leslie 'Terry' Green. Green had worked for the Wiltshaws since October 1950, but had been dismissed on 6 May 1952 after he had taken Wiltshaw's car without permission. Detectives found that Green also had a string of previous convictions for theft, which he had failed to disclose to the Wiltshaws. A visit to his last known address drew a blank. His estranged wife told them she hadn't seen him for a while, but she knew he had been short of money. A visit to all known haunts of Green also failed to unearth the missing

Leslie Terrence 'Terry' Green.
(Author's collection)

chauffer and, believing the man had gone to ground, police named Green as their prime suspect.

As the Scotland Yard detectives went over their evidence, Millen focused on the greatcoat. It seemed likely that the killer had taken it to cover his own clothes which, by virtue of the dreadful injuries he had inflicted on the unfortunate woman, would have been heavily bloodstained. The officers also knew that the killer would probably have subsequently rid himself of the coat, as being found in possession of it would have been enough to hang him.

At the bottom of the Wiltshaw's garden was a path that led towards the railway station at Barlaston and detectives reasoned that the killer would have chosen to escape this way. Millen got in touch with the railway police, who found the missing coat on board the Stafford–Holyhead express.

Detectives built up a picture of their wanted man and found that although he had a wife, he also had a girlfriend, an Irish-born nurse who worked at a hospital in Leeds. It had been to Leeds where Green had driven when he had taken Wiltshaw's car without permission. A check on all tickets issued and submitted on the day of the murder revealed that a ticket issued at Barlaston had been surrendered at Leeds that night. Detectives had copies of the dead woman's rings made up and travelled to Leeds to speak to Green's girlfriend. They showed her the rings and she identified them as ones Green had shown her a few days before.

Satisfied that Green was their man, they issued a photograph to the press and made an announcement that they wished to speak to Green to help them with their enquiries. Seeing his name in the papers, Green thought for a while before surrendering to police at nearby Longton. Green gave a detailed account of his movements on the day of the murder, claiming he was at the Station House Hotel in Leeds at the time of the killing and had witnesses to support this. While it was true he had been seen in the hotel, the manager challenged the times Green had offered to detectives and a rechecking of his movements found that he would have had time to travel to Barlaston, commit the murder and catch the train to Stafford on to Leeds, where he disposed of the bloodstained greatcoat. He mentioned that he had been given the rings he had shown to his girlfriend by two men whom he had met in a café. His alibi did not stand up to close scrutiny and when it was found he had shown the nurse the rings he had claimed to have been given a full day before he claimed to have received them, his alibi was ruined and he was placed under arrest.

Detectives travelled back to the nurse's quarters at Leeds that Green had visited on the night of the murder and, convinced that he had stashed the rings here, they painstakingly searched every inch of the premises. It paid off. Hidden in the coal cellar behind a loose brick several feet off the ground were the missing rings. They were the only items stolen from the house to be recovered.

At Green's trial before Mr Justice Stable at Staffordshire Assizes on 3 December, the evidence against him, circumstantial though it was, was decisive. The gloves found in the Wiltshaws' back garden had a tear in the thumb on the left hand. This matched perfectly with a newly healed scar on Green's hand. Blood found on the inside sleeve of the RAF coat matched a wound on Green's upper arm, and the distinctive marks on the kitchen floor were made by an unusual patterned shoe, identical to a pair Green had purchased on a recent holiday to Spain.

The cellar at Leeds. Green stashed the stolen rings behind the loose bricks beneath the arch at the top.
(TNA: PRO)

Detective Sergeant Ernie Millen's evidence helped secure Green's conviction. (Crime Picture Archive)

On the third day of the trial, as DS Millen prepared to enter the dock, Green whispered to his guards, 'If Ernie Millen gives evidence that hangs me, I'll come back to haunt him!'

'He'd better get in the queue,' Reg Spooner was heard to say when told of Green's comments. With the evidence completed, the jury needed less than half an hour to find Green guilty. He made no appeal and was hanged two days before Christmas.

35

FATE AND THE WEATHER

Frederick Arthur Cross, 26 July 1955

For Frederick Arthur Cross the celebrations of Christmas 1954 had brought devastating news when his wife had told him she was taking their two young children and going to live with her lover in Blaenau Ffestiniog, North Wales. His pleas for her to reconsider went unheeded and as she packed her bags and walked out of their home at Great Haywood, Staffordshire, Cross was distraught.

He spent the early days of January 1955 in an alcohol-induced haze and, after his wife ignored his letters begging her to come home, Cross decided that he had had enough of life and wanted to die. He tried an overdose of sleeping tablets, but this failed and the resulting time off from a local concrete works cost him his job.

Thirty-four-year-old Cross, a Londoner who had moved to the area some years earlier, left the family home and lodged in a hut on a disused RAF base eight miles or so from Uttoxeter. The old timber hut afforded little protection against the biting cold, but it was here that Cross returned to from a trip to Stafford where he purchased some rat-poison with the intention of ending his miserable life. He mixed the poison into a glass of water, but hesitated as he put it to his lips.

Angry at his lack of courage to go through with another attempt at suicide, Cross suddenly had an idea: if he committed a murder and confessed, he would be hanged. This seemed easier than taking his own life and all he would need to do was select a victim and wait for the hangman.

Forty or so miles away, at his home on Dialstone Lane, Stockport, 28-year-old insurance agent Donald Lainton rose early for work and looked out of the window. It was Friday 25 February, and the north of England was in the grip of a fierce blizzard. The road outside was covered in a blanket of snow as Lainton struggled to make his way to work at nearby Marple.

Today Lainton had business to attend to in Sutton Coldfield and although advised not to make the trip, a call to the AA reassured him that the roads were passable. Lainton was making good time when the weather took a turn for the worse and as he passed through Uttoxeter, heavy snowdrifts forced him to pull off the road into the Coach and Horses public house at Great Haywood. Fate and the weather had conspired to introduce him to Frederick Cross.

Entering the quiet inn, Lainton asked to use the telephone. He called the client at Sutton Coldfield and cancelled the appointment, then telephoned the office to say he would be returning once the snowstorm had abated. Finishing with the telephone he ordered a drink and sat down at an empty table. Sitting at the bar, Cross saw Lainton and the two men exchanged greetings. Lainton had enquired about something to eat and when the landlord told him they didn't serve food, Cross said that a pub a little further down the road did serve food and that if he would give him a lift he would point him in the right direction. The two men finished their drinks and walked to the car park.

Cross said to drive in the direction of Uttoxeter, but they had only gone a couple of miles when he told him to turn into a quite lane. Lainton stopped the car and waited for further directions. What happened next was later described by Cross:

> I had a pair of scissors in my mackintosh pocket and I took this out with my right hand and, turning towards him, struck him several blows about the chest and head. I just went berserk. He put his arms up to protect himself, but didn't say a word or call out at all. I cannot remember getting him into the back of the car. All I remember is sitting behind the steering wheel and sweating.

Later that afternoon, a couple walking close to Birchen Bower Farm, Willslock, saw the fawn-coloured Ford Prefect parked up. There was blood on the door handle and, hunched up on the back seat, lay Donald Lainton, dying from his wounds.

Lainton's fawn-coloured Ford Prefect. (TNA: PRO)

Bloodstains in the footwell of Lainton's car. (TNA: PRO)

Staffordshire police were soon at the scene, joined by Professor James Webster of the Home Office Forensic Laboratory at Birmingham. Lainton was rushed to hospital at Stafford as his wife and their young son travelled from Stockport to wait by his bedside, but in the early hours of the following morning, he died.

Police had set up roadblocks and passing drivers were questioned as to whether they had picked up or seen hitchhikers on the roads. It was assumed that robbery had been the motive. It became clear that Lainton hadn't been stabbed on the approach to the farm, rather the crime had been committed further down the road and the killer had dumped the car off the main road while he made his escape. A search of the area found a pair of bloodstained scissors and a number of items belonging to Lainton, including his wallet.

As the search for the killer progressed, Professor Webster carried out his post-mortem. He found that the victim had been stabbed ten times with the scissors. There was a deep cut in the back of the hand, which suggested that Lainton had tried to fend off the blows, but cause of death was from haemorrhage and shock due to the stab wounds, which had lacerated the brain, neck and right lung. There were four main stab wounds – in the neck, head and two in the chest. The most serious was the wound to the head, which had injured the brain, the scissors having been plunged through Lainton's eye socket. Filling in his report, Professor Webster noted that it was incredible that Lainton hadn't been killed outright as it was as vicious an assault as he could recall.

Frederick Cross was arrested in the early hours of Sunday morning. He had travelled down to speak to his mother-in-law at Alcester, from where the police were called and he was brought back to Uttoxeter to face charges. From the outset Cross was clear as to the motive of the crime. 'Let me say that it wasn't robbery,' he told detectives, adding that he had committed the crime so he could be hanged. 'I am not sorry for myself,' he told detectives, 'but I am sorry for him. I wish I had known beforehand that he was married.'

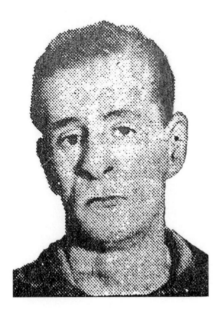

Frederick Cross. (Author's collection)

Professor James Webster, whose expert medical evidence sent numerous men to the gallows at Birmingham. (Crime Picture Archive)

Frederick Arthur Cross stood trial before Mr Justice Gorman at Stafford Assizes on 5 July. He had maintained his refusal for legal aid and entered a plea of guilty after the charge had been read out. The judge told him that legal aid would be available if he so wished and after this was relayed to him by the officer in the dock, Cross again reiterated his plea. 'No sir, I do not want legal aid. I wish to plead guilty.'

'You fully understand don't you, that if you plead "guilty" to this charge I have no alternative but to pass the sentence? Do you fully understand that?' the judge asked.

'Yes, sir,' Cross replied.

The facts of the case were then told to the jury and after just a few minutes the clerk of the court rose to his feet and spoke to Cross: 'You stand convicted on your own confession of wilful murder. Have you anything to say before sentence of death is passed upon you?'

'That is what I wish to be done,' Cross replied, and stood calmly in the dock as Mr Justice Gorman condemned him to death. The whole proceedings had taken just eight minutes.

There was no appeal to the sentence and a date for the execution was fixed for Tuesday 26 July. Cross awaited his chosen fate calmly, but as the date approached the same fear that had prevented him taking the poison six months earlier, returned. After a visit with his mother it was announced that he no longer wanted to be hanged and strenuous efforts were suddenly launched to save him from the hangman.

A petition to the Home Secretary was unable to alter the course of the law, as was a last ditch letter written by his mother to the Queen 'as a mother yourself' to spare her son.

With his courage gone, Cross was a pitiful wreck when the hangmen entered the cell and had to be dragged in terror to the drop, where he duly paid for his horrific and brutal crime.

The LPC4 for Frederick Cross. The governor's praise of Pierrepoint shows they had dealt well with a difficult situation. (Author's collection)

H.M. Prison ......BIRMINGHAM...

........5th July...............1955...........

Register No. ....543............Name .Frederick Arthur CROSS...............................

Court and Place ..Assizes.Stafford,...

Date ....30/6.-.5.7.55...

Crime ....Murder,...

Date of reception on conviction......5th.July,.1955,...................................

Probable date of carrying out sentence ....26th.July,.1955..(will.be.confirmed

---

1.

GENTLEMEN,

I beg to report that the above-named prisoner has been received into this prison under sentence of death, and to request that I may be furnished with the list of candidates reported to be competent for the office of executioner, together with copies of the records as to the conduct and efficiency of each of them, with a view to their transmission to the High Sheriff, as directed in Standing Orders. I beg also to apply for a copy of the memorandum of instructions for carrying out the details of an execution ; also for a copy of the table of drops.

I am, Gentlemen,
Your obedient Servant,

To
The Prison Commissioners.

....
Governor.

2.

The Governor,

.......................BIRMINGHAM.........Prison.

(1) *Your attention is specially directed to the Memorandum, dated 26/10/36, in* the enclosed packet of forms, and also to Standing Order 170(2). Any unused forms should be returned to this office.

The object of supplying the information to the Secretary of State is to help in reviewing the case. Everything should be done, therefore, to supply every detail ; and the Medical Officer should report on the mental and physical condition of the prisoner while under his observation, calling attention to anything which may have been brought forward at the trial bearing on the prisoner's condition.

The Commissioners desire you personally to satisfy yourself that the instructions are carefully and promptly carried out in every detail.

(2) The services of *H. Harry B. ALLEN* are recommended for employment as Assistant Executioner.

(3) If the execution is to take place at 9 a.m., the Commissioners request that you will arrange for the usual prison routine to be followed during the time of execution so that prisoners will be scattered over the prison at their respective tasks. Their minds will be occupied ; and any noise caused by the trap-doors should pass unnoticed.

[P.T.O.

Prison commissioners' official memorandum relating to the execution of Frederick Arthur
Cross. (Author's collection)

2

The following arrangements are suggested :—

Early morning exercise as usual ; associated labour at 8.35 a.m. Prisoners normally employed near the execution shed given a period of additional exercise in a yard remote from it and the prison clock chime disconnected for the hour of nine. The executioners lodged so that they neither have to enter the prison nor cross the yards.

(4) If the Medical Officer considers any Young Prisoner in your custody is likely to be affected adversely by the execution, he should submit a report on the prisoner stating fully his reasons for such an opinion in order that the Commissioners may consider the advisability of transferring the prisoner.

Please inform the Assistant Executioner that he will be eligible for reasonable travelling expenses. Taxi fares will only be payable when public transport is not available.

With reference to A.1939/86 dated 11.1.55 please note that during the past twelve months Mr. A. Pierrepoint has been employed .8...times and Mr. S. Wade ..3...times.

for Establishment Officer.

F 274.

3.

The Commissioners.

Noted. The execution was carried at 9.30.a.m. today.

Unused Forms are returned herewith.

Newspaper reports of the execution and inquest, if reported, will be forwarded in due course.

Governor,
Birmingham Prison.
26th July 1955.

Prison commissioners' official memorandum relating to the execution of Frederick Arthur Cross (continued from previous page). (Author's collection)

Mothers with young children were among people outside Winson Green Prison to read the notice posted after the execution.

Man who wanted to die is hanged at Birmingham prison

Frederick Arthur Cross, 33-year-old labourer, of Hillside, Farley, Great Haywood, near Stafford, was hanged a Winson Green Prison today for the murder of Stockpor insurance agent Donald Haywood Lainton (aged 28).

Cross's execution made the headlines in that evening's newspapers. (Author's collection)

36

NEGLECTING HER DUTY

Corbett Montague Roberts, 2 August 1955

'I entirely leave myself in your hands. I entitle you to take my life.'

Confession by Corbett Montague Roberts, 31 May 1955

'I have done my wife in,' the man told the startled desk sergeant as he walked into Aston police station, Birmingham. It was 8.40 a.m., Tuesday, 31 May 1955. The man gave his name as Corbett Montague Roberts and said that he was 46-year-old Jamaican born, unemployed and resided at 113 Frederick Road, Aston. Roberts then told the startled detectives, in precise detail, the events that had led to his confession. Officers hurried to his house to find that Roberts had been telling the truth.

Cautioned, Roberts said that a few days earlier, at a family gathering, some money had gone missing and he had been accused of taking it. He said that his 41-year-old wife, Doris, far from backing him up, had neglected her duty as a wife and, instead of offering her support, had accused him of taking it.

That morning, a small sum of money had been left on the breakfast table, which Roberts planned to use for his pocketmoney and bus fares. He said that as he reached out to take it, his wife snatched it up and put it into her purse.

He demanded that she hand it over and, refusing, she mocked, 'You will have to kill me for that money!' She had then dropped the purse down her blouse. They began to quarrel and in a rage Roberts picked up a hammer and battered her repeatedly about the head. So enraged was he, that when the shaft on the hammer broke, he stopped, located another hammer in his toolbox, and continued with the frightful assault. Then, satisfied his wife was dead, Roberts placed the hammer onto a table and calmly walked to the local police station and gave himself up.

He pleaded guilty at his trial before Mr Justice Gorman at Birmingham Assizes on 15 July and said that his life was forfeit. Roberts said that he had never intended to kill his wife but he had done so in a moment of passion. He refused legal aid, stating, 'I'm not interested, because I am guilty.'

Once sentence of death had been passed he told his solicitor that he wanted none of his family to benefit from the sale of his property and that it should go to an old people's home. The case was considered by the Home Office, with a view to granting the prisoner a reprieve, but the file noted the killer's previous brutality to his wife and the horrific nature of the attack. One official noted on the file that Corbett was 'of little use to the world' and the law was allowed to take its course.

The front room of Roberts's house, Frederick Road, Aston. (TNA: PRO)

Doris Roberts lies dead on the kitchen floor. (TNA: PRO)

Reference_____ 1731/15

This Jamaican beat his wife on the head with a hammer until the shaft broke & then went on with a second hammer: he then gave himself up to the police. At present he insists on pleading guilty.

17.6.55.

Seen thanks   It appears that this man has always been violent towards his wife. This violence being apparently born of jealousy.   He is of little use to the world.

17/6/55.

seen, thanks.

17: vi. 55

Will you please instruct Pugh to act as our Agent in this case

8.6.55

When considering whether to reprieve Corbett Roberts his previous record was taken into consideration. On the file it was noted that the Jamaican was 'of little use to the world'. (Author's collection)

Justice in this case was swift, with Corbett Roberts being hanged just nine weeks to the day since he had brutally murdered his wife.

37

CHILD-KILLER

Ernest Charles Harding, 9 August 1955

At 4 o'clock on Wednesday, 8 June 1955, 10-year-old schoolgirl Evelyn Patricia Higgins finished her lessons at the Frederick Bird Primary School, Coventry, and hurried to a local hairdresser's, where she had an appointment. An hour later, her hair washed and cut, she left the salon and made her way back to her home at 26 Lowther Street, just a short walk from the school. She never arrived.

Her worried parents contacted a number of school friends and, when this drew a blank, they searched the local streets before calling the police. Officers investigating her disappearance soon spoke to two teenage girls, who told them of a man that had tried to lure them into a car on the afternoon Evelyn disappeared. They had refused his advances and were able to give a detailed description of the man, who they said had light brown hair going grey and was aged about 40. They were also able to give a description of the car, which they described as a black, two-door saloon.

Another witness, a cyclist, had also seen the driver talking to the young girls and was able to give officers a more detailed description of the car. He said it was a black, two-door Standard 9 saloon, and from the registration plate it was either a 1937 or 1938 model. There was also a small Union Jack flag painted on the bonnet.

A description of the car was published in local papers and investigations soon led police to Ernest Charles Harding, a 42-year-old bricklayer who lived at Lauderdale Avenue, Coventry. Harding had also read the reports of the investigation and, fearing that the police were onto him, he drove to a field at nearby Stretton-on-Dunsmore, where, on Saturday 11 June, he fixed a pipe to the exhaust of the car and attempted to commit suicide.

Officers arrived in the nick of time and, thwarted in his efforts, Harding was taken into custody, where he made a number of conflicting statements. Firstly he claimed to have been at the cinema at the time Evelyn had disappeared. This was soon found to be untrue. He then admitted that he had indeed picked up Evelyn and she had travelled with him in his car, but he had no recollection of anything happening until he had noticed her dead body. Harding said he had a spade in the car, and in a panic he drove to woodland near Coleshill, where he had buried the body in a shallow grave. Detectives searched the woods at Coleshill on the following day and discovered Evelyn's body as Harding described.

Evelyn had been concealed beneath 8 inches of earth and a post-mortem found that cause of death was a stab wound to the throat. There were also signs of attempted

Harding's black, two-door Standard 9. (TNA: PRO)

Evelyn Higgins. (T.J. Leech Archive)

Evelyn Higgins disappeared after leaving Frederick Bird Primary School on 8 June 1955. (Crime Picture Archive)

suffocation and she had been sexually assaulted. Harding admitted to trying to have sex with the young girl and claimed he had put his hand over her mouth to stifle her cries, but he maintained he had no memory of anything else, especially the use of a knife.

Ernest Harding offered a defence of insanity when he appeared before by Mr Justice Lynskey at Birmingham on 21 July. His counsel claimed that Harding had suffered a head injury in 1952 and this had caused him to become moody and bad-tempered. Harding was a married man with two grown-up children. His wife told the court that since the accident, in which Harding had sustained a fractured skull, he suffered blackouts, which would leave him with no memory of what he had done. She said that on the night of Evelyn's disappearance, Harding had returned home at 7.15 p.m. and his behaviour had been quite normal.

The medical evidence was debated in court. Psychiatrist Dr Arthur Hale, called by the defence, told the court that Harding had probably been aware of what he was doing during the abduction and assault but not during the killing. Dr Percy Coats, medical officer at Winson Green Gaol, refuted this and said that during his observations of the prisoner, Harding had appeared perfectly sane at all times. The prosecution pointed out that Harding himself had made no mention of his head injuries whilst being interviewed and the defence had only chose this as a weak defence to the murder charge once the case came to court.

Satisfied that Harding had been fully aware of what he had been doing during the brutal assault, the jury took just a short time to find that he was guilty of murder and he was duly convicted. He was hanged by Steve Wade on 9 August 1955.

Hangman Steve Wade carried out just one more execution after he hanged Harding at Birmingham on 9 August 1955. (Author's collection)

NOTE

Nowadays, whenever a child murder hits the headlines, there are often campaigns in newspaper to bring back the death penalty for the perpetrators of such despicable crimes. It is, perhaps, strange then to find that following the passing of the Homicide Act in 1957 certain kinds of crimes were 'downgraded' to non-capital murder and as such would not be liable to the death penalty. The murder of a child was deemed no longer worthy of the ultimate penalty. Thus, in August 1955, Ernest Harding became the last man hanged in Great Britain for the murder of a child.

'Capital Punishment Amendment Act, 1868'

(31 & 32 *Vict. c.* 24, *s.* 7)

The sentence of the law passed

upon ~~ERNEST CHARLES HARDING~~

found guilty of murder, will be

carried into execution at 9.30 a.m.

to-morrow.

ST. Wade _____ Sheriff of *Warwickshire.*

A'Kenyon _____ Governor.

8th August. ____ 19 55

~~BIRMINGHAM~~ Prison.

No. 278

Above: *Notice of execution posted on the prison gates (Author's collection)*

Left: *Ernest Harding, the last man to be hanged in Great Britain for child murder. (T.J. Leech Archive)*

Records of an Execution carried out in *Birmingham* Prison on the *8th August* 1955					
Particulars of the condemned Prisoner.	Particulars of the Execution.		Remarks respecting the Executioner and his Assistants (if any).		
			Name and Address, in full, of the Executioner.	Name and Address, in full, of the 1st Assistant to the Executioner (if any).	Name and Address, in full, of the 2nd Assistant to the Executioner (if any).
Ernest Charles HARDING	The length of the drop, as determined before the execution. 6 feet 6 inches.		*S. Wade* *Edendale* *Amcott Road* *Edenborfe* *N'd Humbr*	*R.L. Stewart* *58 Bridgematic Street* *Oldham* *Lancs*	
1591	The length of the drop, as measured after the execution, from the level of the floor of the scaffold to the heels of the suspended culprit. 6 feet 8½ inches.				
Male	Cause of death [(a) Dislocation of vertebrae, (b) Asphyxia.] *Fracture dislocation of cervical vertebrae*	OPINION of the Governor and Medical Officer as to the manner in which each of the above-named persons has performed his duty.			
42		1. Has he performed his duty satisfactorily?	1. *Yes*	1. *Yes*	1.
5 feet 5½ inches	Approximate statement of the character and amount of destruction to the soft and bony structures of the neck.	2. Was his general demeanour satisfactory during the period that he was in the prison, and does he appear to be a respectable person?	2. *Yes*	2. *Yes*	2.
Stocky	*Fracture dislocation with bruising of soft tissues*	3. Has he shown capacity, both physical and mental, for the duty, and general suitability for the post?	3. *Yes (see 5)*	3. *Yes*	3.
		4. Is there any ground for supposing that he will bring discredit upon his office by lecturing, or by granting interviews to persons who may seek to elicit information from him in regard to the execution or by any other act?	4. *No*	4. *No*	4.
175	If there were any peculiarities in the build or condition of the prisoner, or in the structure of his neck, which necessitated a departure from the scale of drops, particulars should be stated.	5. Are you aware of any circumstances occurring before, at, or after the execution which tend to show that he is not a suitable person to employ on future occasions either on account of incapacity for performing the duty, or the likelihood of his creating public scandal before or after an execution?	5. *Seems to have defective eyesight*	5. *No*	5.
Muscular	None	↑			*H'Kenyon*

LPC4 notes the governor's concern that Wade's eyesight is failing. He was later dismissed on medical grounds 'as a precaution against what may happen due to his failing eyesight, not because of it.' (Author's collection)

38

IN THE FURTHERANCE OF THEFT

Dennis Howard, 4 December 1957

Guns fascinated Dennis Howard. A keen collector, 24-year-old Howard, an unemployed labourer from Smethwick had, over the years, acquired a varied armoury of pistols and ammunition. On Friday, 17 May 1957, Howard slipped one of those guns, a Mauser automatic, into his pocket and travelled into Dudley.

At 5.25 p.m. that afternoon, just before closing time, he entered 'Halford', a gent's outfitter's shop on Wolverhampton Street, and asked the proprietor, 21-year-old David Alan Keasey, if he could try on a sweater from the shelf behind the counter. Keasey shrewdly viewed the customer. The jumper was more expensive than one the average working man would probably opt for, but nevertheless he handed the garment over for the man to examine.

Keasey's suspicions were proved correct when the customer made to bolt for the door. Suspecting something like this, the shopkeeper intercepted him and jammed his foot against the door. It was then that Howard pulled out the gun and, waving it menacingly, ordering Keasey to get back. Keasey was not about to meekly hand over his stock and lunged at the gunman. They began a struggle which spilled over into the doorway. A shot rang out and Keasey slumped to the ground.

Across the street, 15-year-old David Hiscox thought he heard a car backfiring, and as he looked round he saw a man fleeing from the shop shouting that a man has just had a fit. Passers-by gathered around the stricken man just as 19-year-old Doreen Bell, Keasey's fiancée who had arranged to meet him after work, approached the shop. Puzzled at the crowd, she quickened her step and arrived moments before the ambulance. Keasey was removed to hospital at Dudley, where the full horror of what happened that afternoon was revealed. Rather than having a fit or seizure – which the ambulance men had been initially told by those at the scene – Keasey, certified dead on arrival, had died from a single gunshot to the back.

The Chief Constable of Warwickshire requested the assistance of Scotland Yard and two senior detectives were soon at the scene. The wanted man was described as in his mid-twenties, fair-haired, 5ft 10ins tall, medium build, wearing a fawn raglan-sleeved raincoat and speaking with a local accent. The gun found at the scene of the murder had a thumbprint on the trigger, but it did not match any prints on file. Officers questioned shoppers who had been on Wolverhampton Street that afternoon, along with bus and taxi drivers who had been in the vicinity of the murder, but without success.

'Halford' gent's outfitters, Wolverhampton Street, Dudley. (TNA: PRO)

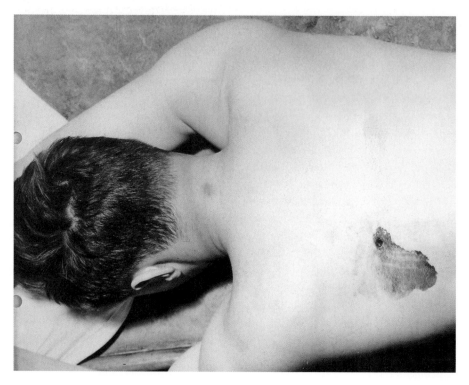

Keasey was killed by a single shot to the back. (TNA: PRO)

David Keasey and Doreen Bell had been due to marry on 11 June, and on this date detectives called a press conference, asking members of the public to be alert to anyone who had changed their habits or began acting differently since the murder had taken place.

Dennis Howard was eventually arrested on Monday 24 June. He had discussed the shooting with a friend and what he had said was enough for the friend to contact the police. Although he readily admitted stealing the sweater, and that the gun that killed Keasey was cocked, he claimed the shooting had been accidental and that the pistol had discharged inadvertently during the struggle. Howard claimed Keasey had grabbed the gun and pulled it towards him, causing it to go off accidentally.

Despite Howard's claim that the killing was an accident, he was charged with capital murder, in the furtherance of theft, by shooting, and was sent for trial at the Worcestershire Assizes in October before Mr Justice Hinchcliffe. George Baker QC, leading for the prosecution, said Howard's crime was an intentional killing: 'Keasey got in his way and would not let him commit robbery ... Howard, in danger of being caught, fired the gun.'

Howard's counsel disputed the premeditation and claimed that although the accused had left home with a pistol and three rounds of ammunition, he had only decided to rob on impulse. He cocked the gun, but could not remember whether the

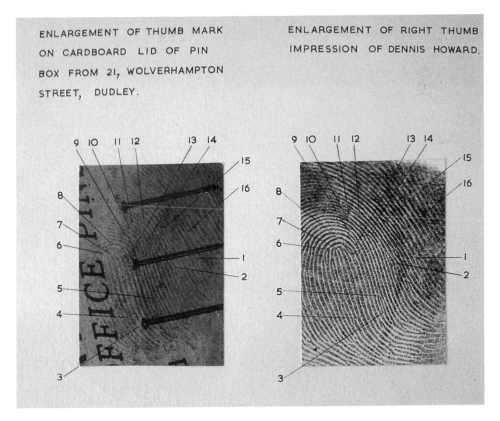

ENLARGEMENT OF THUMB MARK ON CARDBOARD LID OF PIN BOX FROM 21, WOLVERHAMPTON STREET, DUDLEY.

ENLARGEMENT OF RIGHT THUMB IMPRESSION OF DENNIS HOWARD.

Howard's fingerprints were found at the scene of the crime. (Author's collection)

Doreen Bell arrived at the shop just after her fiancé had been shot. (TNA: PRO)

safety catch was on or off. Howard gave evidence to the court in which he gave his version of events:

> I thought it would frighten the fellow behind the counter to hand over some money without any trouble. By trouble I mean no fighting. I did not intend to fire the gun, even if the fellow caused trouble. He went into the back of the shop with something in his hand. He saw I'd pulled a gun out of my pocket. I told him the gun was loaded and he said something about 'don't be silly'. I thought he was going to run out. He ran around after me, grabbing my arm, and we started to struggle. I was still holding the pistol. It all happened in a flash. I can't explain what really happened. All I wanted to do was get loose.

The pathologist who had conducted the post-mortem told the court that Keasey had been killed by a bullet through the heart, which had entered through his back. Howard told the court he had never seen Keasey before that afternoon and he had no desire to kill or seriously harm him.

Tellingly, the prosecution read out to the court Howard's initial statement to the police, in which expressed no regret for the killing, only that he had been caught, and seemed intent on blaming Keasey for causing his own death.

In his final address, Howard's counsel said that the accused had no intention of killing Keasey and told the jury they would be doing their duty 'if you said he was not guilty of capital murder.'

Summing-up, the judge spoke of the defence of manslaughter. He told the jury that for it to be proven, the gun must have been discharged by a complete accident, but that if Howard had pulled the trigger intentionally, then that was murder. He pointed out that Howard had admitted to cocking the trigger. This, the judge told the jury, in his opinion, suggested that a verdict of manslaughter would be unjust and that they, the jury, should not be frightened of a verdict of murder.

Mindful of the recently passed Homicide Act, which categorised types of murder liable to the death penalty, and aware that if convicted Howard faced execution, the judge addressed the jury:

'It would be utterly wrong of you to return a verdict of manslaughter just because you don't like the sound of murder. Justice could not be done in this country if juries were looking over their shoulders, wondering what the result of their verdict might be.'

On Friday 18 October, Dennis Howard was found guilty of murder and informed he would 'suffer death in the manner authorised by law.' Asked if he wished to say anything why sentence of death should not be passed on him, Howard calmly replied, 'No, sir.'

Hangman Harry Allen carried out three executions at Birmingham in the post-Homicide Act era. (Author's collection)

A date of Wednesday 6 November, was set for the execution but this was postponed when Howard appealed. On 19 November, the Court of Criminal Appeal, headed by Lord Chief Justice Goddard, dismissed the appeal, saying that it could not be disputed that the killing was planned, in the sense that Howard pulled the trigger, and from that the law implied that he either intended to kill or cause Keasey grievous bodily harm. It could not be an accident, as the gun was cocked. The appeal was dismissed, as was a further appeal to the House of Lords.

At 9.30 a.m. on Tuesday 4 December, Dennis Howard was hanged. He was the second man to die on the gallows in England since the 1957 Homicide Act had been passed. By coincidence, the other executed man, Carlisle murderer John Willson Vickers, hanged at Durham, had also been sentenced to death by Mr Justice Hinchcliffe.

39

FOR A POUND OR A FEW SHILLINGS

Matthew Kavanagh, 12 August 1958

In the spring of 1958, 32-year-old Irish born labourer Matthew Kavanagh moved into lodgings on Hillmorton Road, Rugby. A short time later he lost his job with the English Electric Co. and, when he could no longer pay his rent, he was told to find somewhere else to live.

On Saturday 12 April, Kavanagh was out drinking and later returned to the boarding house on Hillmorton Road where he met up with Isaiah Dixon, a 60-year-old clerk with the Ministry of Transport. Dixon was very drunk and Kavanagh offered to help him upstairs to his room. He then strangled Dixon with the man's own black silk tie, before stealing cash from his wallet. Later that evening, himself now quite drunk, Kavanagh went into a café in Coventry and told the owner, 'I'm in trouble. I've killed a man.'

Interviewed by police officers, Kavanagh said he was blind-drunk when it had happened and that he 'might have taken from him for a pound or a few shillings.' He said that Dixon was also drunk and had asked Kavanagh to help him to his room. Kavanagh then claimed, 'I did not know what I was doing ... I strangled him with his own tie. I went through his pockets and took four pounds in notes and some silver.'

Kavanagh was then charged with murder, his second murder charge in less than a year. In 1957 he had been charged with the non-capital murder of a married woman, with whom he had been associating. In June, the police had been called to the British

Matthew Kavanagh.
(T.J. Leech Archive)

Legion Club in Coventry Road, Birmingham in answer to a mysterious 999 call, which
the caller referred to as the 'Sheldon Affair'. The male caller spoke of a body on some
nearby wasteland by the Wheatsheaf hotel in Sheldon, and said the deceased was 35-year-
old Evelyn Ulla, the estranged wife of an Indian seaman employed at Winson Green
Prison as a stoker.

Officers discovered the woman's body in tall grass on her back, with her arms folded
over her chest. The post-mortem revealed she had died of vagal inhibition, or momentary
pressure on the nerve of the neck, which produced heart failure. Very occasionally intense
sexual intercourse can cause this. The caller gave his name as Matthew Kavanagh and he
seemed so genuinely distressed at the woman's death that detectives did not immediately
suspect murder. Kavanagh said he had known the woman for a couple of weeks and, after

leaving a pub, they had gone to the wasteland to be alone. Mrs Ulla complained of being cold, so Kavanagh offered to pull her scarf tighter around her neck. There was no struggle and she died instantly. He told police he was unable to believe she was dead and he did his best to revive her.

He was charged with non-capital murder and when he appeared before Solihull magistrates Kavanagh wore a black armband through proceedings. At the committal proceedings the charge had been reduced to manslaughter and at the Warwickshire Assizes that July the court heard how the woman suffered from a rare medical condition, which would explain how even the slightest pressure on her neck could be fatal, and Kavanagh was acquitted.

For his second murder trial Kavanagh appeared before Mr Justice Streatfeild at the Warwickshire Assizes. This time the charge was capital murder, in the furtherance of theft, of Isaiah Dixon. Kavanagh's confession to theft along with the admission to strangling Dixon was to have serious implications, as, following the passing of the Homicide Act in 1957, only a handful of crimes now carried the death penalty, one of which was murder during or in the furtherance of theft.

Kavanagh's defence claimed that the killing was an accident and at the most manslaughter, but although the jury knew nothing of his previous murder charge, they only took forty minutes to convict him of Dixon's murder. The Court of Criminal Appeal rejected his appeal at the end of July; having twice been charged with murder in less than a year, this factor probably weighed heavily against Kavanagh when the Home Secretary pondered his decision whether or not to reprieve him.

40

A WORTHLESS ALIBI

Oswald Augustus Grey, 20 November 1962

Shortly after 6.30 p.m. on Saturday, 3 June 1962, 47-year-old Thomas Bates was shot dead behind the counter of his newsagent's shop at 176 Lee Bank Road, Edgbaston, Birmingham. His aged mother, hearing the single gunshot, came hurrying down from the living quarters above the shop and found her son slumped on the floor with a 7.65 Walther automatic revolver beside the body.

At that same moment, neighbour Mrs Margaret Bradley was standing at a bus stop on Lee Bank Road when she heard what she thought was a car engine backfiring and, as she turned, she noticed a man leave the newsagents shop and head down the street. She later told detectives the man was either dark skinned or covered in oil, like a mechanic or miner may appear after finishing work.

Bates's newsagents, Lee Bank Road, Edgbaston. (Author's collection)

Detectives questioned a number of Jamaicans in the area, one of whom was 19-year-old Oswald Grey, an unemployed baker who lived at 47 Cannon Hill Road, Balsall Heath. Theft or attempted theft was believed to be the motive for the crime and Grey was known to be short of money and had been claiming National Assistance for over a year. After initially denying owning a gun, he then admitted that he had once owned a revolver of the same type as that used to kill Thomas Bates, which he admitted he had stolen, but claimed that on the afternoon of the murder he had met a man he knew as 'Mover' at a café in Mary Street and lent him the gun. The man had then returned the gun to him late on the night of the murder.

'Mover' was tracked down and was found to be one Harris Karnfi, but he denied ever meeting Grey and had certainly not borrowed a gun from him. Crucially, he also had witnesses, two sisters, who both swore that Karnfi had been in their company from 11 a.m. on the Saturday morning, until gone ten o'clock that same night.

All told, during various interviews with detectives Grey gave five different accounts of who had the gun at the time of the killing. Satisfied he was the guilty man, Grey was charged two days later.

Before Mr Justice Paull at Warwickshire Assizes in Birmingham, on Wednesday 10 October, Grey was charged with capital murder, by shooting, in the furtherance of theft. During the trial Grey admitted being in possession of the murder weapon at 3.30 p.m. on the afternoon of the murder, and at 10 p.m. at night, however he denied shooting Mr Bates at 6.30 p.m.

His defence offered an alibi that, at the time of the shooting, Grey was with his father and a female friend of his father's. They had visited a pub together and at the time of the shooting, the three of them had been in Church Street together. Both

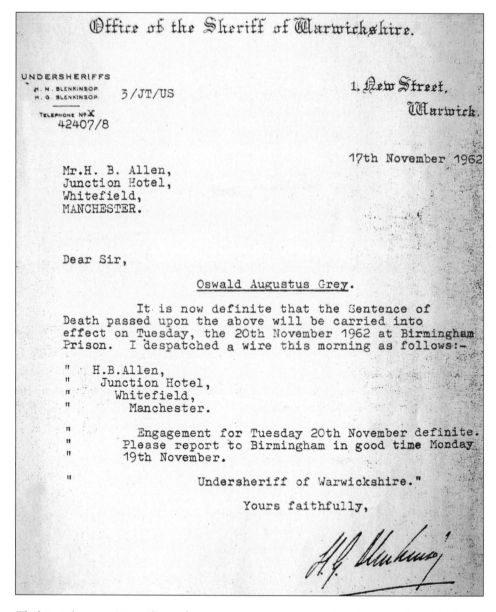

Office of the Sheriff of Warwickshire.

UNDERSHERIFFS
H. M. BLENKINSOP.
H. G. BLENKINSOP.   3/JT/US

TELEPHONE Nº X
42407/8

1, New Street,
Warwick.

17th November 1962

Mr.H. B. Allen,
Junction Hotel,
Whitefield,
MANCHESTER.

Dear Sir,

                    Oswald Augustus Grey.

        It is now definite that the Sentence of
Death passed upon the above will be carried into
effect on Tuesday, the 20th November 1962 at Birmingham
Prison. I despatched a wire this morning as follows:-

"   H.B.Allen,
"   Junction Hotel,
"   Whitefield,
"   Manchester.

"   Engagement for Tuesday 20th November definite.
"   Please report to Birmingham in good time Monday
"   19th November.

"   Undersheriff of Warwickshire."

            Yours faithfully,

The letter to hangman Harry Allen confirming that Grey's execution would go ahead. (Author's collection)

Grey's father and the woman confirmed they had spent time with Grey but as neither could confirm the exact times they were together, and with no supporting evidence, it made the alibi worthless. The defence also called Margaret Bradley, who swore that the man she had seen exiting the shop shortly after hearing the shooting was not Oswald Grey.

The prosecution claimed that Grey's account of lending the gun was pure fabrication and called to the stand the café owners, who both testified that Grey had not been on their premises on the day of the murder.

Staff Detail for Tuesday 20th November, 1962.

```
6.15 a.m.    Prison Unlocked.   F.O.W. etc. on duty.
6.40 a.m.    Staff on Duty.  Slop out.    Serve Breakfasts.
6.50 a.m.    Discharges etc. to Reception.
7.30 a.m.    Discharges Out.  All escorts out by 7.40 a.m.
7.30 a.m.    All Inmates locked up and accounted for
             Officers to patrol Landings and Yards as detailed.
8.10 a.m.    Staff to Breakfast
9.10 a.m.    Staff Return.   Inmates to work (all Red Bands etc. to Shops)
11.30 a.m.   Dinners served.
12.0 p.m.    Staff to Dinner.
1.30 p.m.    Staff Return  (Normal Working)
4.40 p.m.    Teas served.
5.10 p.m.    Staff off Duty.
```

All Staff normally on duty at 8.0 a.m. to commence 8.15 a.m.

Sick Parade to take place in Hospital.

Farm Party, Works Party, Stores, to work about 8.30 a.m. and work as instructed.

P.O.   On duty 7.40 a.m. i/c C.2. will allow no unauthorised persons to enter the Wing until Execution is completed and Condemned Cell locked up.

Offr.   On duty 7.40 a.m. will patrol outside C. Wing until body is removed to Mortuary.   No unauthorised person to enter this area.

Offr.   On duty 7.40 a.m. will patrol Main Drive (Gate End), will allow no movement between 7.40 and 8.15 a.m., also when body is removed to Mortuary and from Mortuary for burial.

Offr.   On duty 7.40 a.m. will patrol Main Drive (Officers' Mess End) Instructions as for Officer at Gate End.

Offr.   Will meet Executioners and attend them until departure.

Offrs.   Will take over duty in Condemned Cell at 6.40 a.m. and escort inmate to Scaffold.

   No person will be allowed to enter the Prison from 7.45 a.m. until Execution is over and Staff depart to Breakfast.

                Will meet High Sheriff and conduct to Governor's office.

                The Inquest will be at 10.30 a.m.

Prison detail on the day of Grey's execution. (Author's collection)

H.M.P.Birmingham,
13.11.62

Detail for WORKS STAFF on Tuesday 20th Nov. 1962

6.15 a.m.   On duty. Staff as detailed by F.o.W.. Enter chamber by C.1.
             entrance.

6.25 a.m.   Executioner collected by F.o.W. Set up under his instructions.
             He then returns to breakfast at approx 6.45.a.m.

6.45 a.m.   Main discipline staff on duty.

7.50 a.m.   Staff as needed to take up positions.

8.20 a.m.   (approx) Remove body. Repack boxes. Lock up. Prepare for
             inquest.

10.50 a.m.   Identification and viewing by jury if required.

11.05 a.m.   Remove body to old dental surgery.

11.45 a.m.   F.O.W. to collect Chaplain and body to be removed from
             dental surgery to burial ground.

12.00 noon. Service and Internment.

Note

Main drive to be clear from 11.10 a.m. to approx 11.15 a.m.

Reception to be clear from 10.55 a.m. as required

Mess and Hospital Ward to be clear from 11.40 until

about 11.50 a.m.

Foreman of Works' memo for the execution of Oswald Grey, November 1962. (Author's collection)

With evidence linking him to the gun, a motive for the attempted robbery in being short of cash, and a worthless alibi, the three-day trial ended with Grey being convicted and sentenced to death. His execution was set for 30 October but he lodged an unsuccessful appeal that put the execution back a further three weeks.

Grey spent the six weeks in the death-cell limbo dancing and hand jiving, reputedly indifferent to his fate. On Tuesday 20 November Oswald Augustus Grey, now aged just 20 years old, was led to the gallows and became the last man to be hanged at Birmingham.

APPENDIX

PRIVATE EXECUTIONS AT BIRMINGHAM
1885–1962

Date	Convict	Executioner	Assistant (s)
17 March 1885	Henry Kimberley	James Berry	None engaged
28 August 1888 +	George Nathaniel Daniels Henry Benjamin Jones	James Berry	None engaged
26 August 1890	Frederick Davies	James Berry	None engaged
4 April 1894	Frederick William Fenton	James Billington	None engaged
18 August 1896	Frank Taylor	James Billington	None engaged
20 August 1901	John Joyce	James Billington	William Billington
5 April 1904	Charles Samuel Dyer	William Billington	John Billington
16 August 1904	Samuel Holden	William Billington	John Ellis
13 August 1913	Frank Greening	Thomas Pierrepoint	George Brown
16 August 1916	William Alan Butler	John Ellis	Edward Taylor
9 April 1918	Louis Van der Kerkhove	John Ellis	George Brown
8 August 1919	Henry Thomas Gaskin	John Ellis	Edward Taylor
30 December 1920	Samuel Westwood	John Ellis	None engaged

Date	Convict	Executioner	Assistant (s)
22 December 1921	Edward O'Connor	John Ellis	Robert Wilson
11 August 1922	Elijah Poutney	John Ellis	Robert Baxter
19 December 1922	William Rider	John Ellis	William Willis
5 January 1926	John Fisher	William Willis	Robert Wilson
13 April 1926	George Sharpes	William Willis	Robert Baxter
31 January 1928	James Joseph Power	Thomas Pierrepoint	Robert Wilson
3 January 1931	Victor Edward Betts	Thomas Pierrepoint	Alfred Allen
2 February 1933	Jeremiah Hanbury	Thomas Pierrepoint	Robert Wilson Albert Pierrepoint*
28 December 1933	Stanley Eric Hobday	Thomas Pierrepoint	Albert Pierrepoint
16 April 1936	Dorothea N. Waddingham	Thomas Pierrepoint	Albert Pierrepoint
7 February 1940	Peter Barnes James Richards	Thomas Pierrepoint	Thomas Phillips Albert Pierrepoint Stanley Cross
19 September 1941	Eli Richards	Thomas Pierrepoint	Stanley Cross
30 January 1942	Arthur Peach	Thomas Pierrepoint	Henry Critchell
10 September 1942	Harold Oswald Merry	Thomas Pierrepoint	Henry Critchell
3 August 1943	William Quayle	Thomas Pierrepoint	Alex Riley
29 March 1949	James Farrell	Albert Pierrepoint	Harry Kirk Sydney Dernley* Herbert Allen* George Dickinson*
29 March 1950	Piotr Makskimowski	Albert Pierrepoint	Sydney Dernley
3 April 1951	William Arthur Watkins	Albert Pierrepoint	Harry B. Allen

Date	Convict	Executioner	Assistant (s)
1 January 1952	Horace Carter	Albert Pierrepoint	Sydney Dernley
23 December 1952	Leslie Terrence Green	Albert Pierrepoint	Sydney Dernley
26 July 1955	Frederick Arthur Cross	Albert Pierrepoint	Harry B. Allen
2 August 1955	Corbett Montague Roberts	Stephen Wade	Harry B. Allen
9 August 1955	Ernest Charles Harding	Stephen Wade	Robert L. Stewart
4 December 1957	Dennis Howard	Harry B. Allen	Royston L. Rickard Thomas Cunliffe* Harry F. Robertson*
12 August 1958	Matthew Kavanagh	Harry B. Allen	Thomas Cunliffe
20 November 1962	Oswald Augustus Grey	Harry B Allen	Samuel Plant

* Present as a non-participating observer

+ signifies a double execution of prisoners not connected and hanged for seperate crimes

INDEX

Dowd, Charles 75
Dutton, Jessie 66
Dyer, Charles Samuel (aka Hammond) 40

Eardley, Bert 79
Elborough, Florence Nightingale 31
Ellis, John 16, 54, 58

Farrell, James 18, 108
Fenton, Frederick William 31
Field, Mr Justice 22
Finnemore, Mr Justice 118
Fisher, John 66
Fox, Charles 83
Fox, Gladys 83
Freeman, Harriet 63
Freeman, Rachael 63

Gaskin, Henry Thomas 51
Gaskin, Lizzie 51
Gentle, Rex 96
Goddard, Mr (later Lord Chief) Justice 92, 148
Gorman, Mr Justice 131, 135
Green, Leslie Terrence 124
Greening, Frank 43
Grey, Oswald Augustus 150
Griffiths, Frances 46

Hale, Dr Arthur 140
Hanbury, Jeremiah 78
Harding, Ernest 16, 138
Harris, Florence Mabel 27
Harris, George Richard 26
Harris, Sarah Annie 27
Harris, William 27
Hastings Louisa 24
Hastings, Alice 24
Hastings, Emma 24
Hastings, William 24
Hawkins, Mr Justice 30
Herne, Elizabeth 43
Hewitt, Joseph 93
Hewitt, Mary 93
Higgins, Evelyn Patricia 138
Hill, Daniel R. 9
Hinchcliffe, Mr Justice 145
Hiscox, Daniel 143

Hobday, Stanley Eric 82
Holden, Samuel 42
Howard, Dennis 18, 143
Humphreys, Mr Justice 79
Humphries, Susan 43

Jones, Det. Con. Henry 44
Jones, Henry Benjamin 26
Joyce, John 39

Karnfi, Harris 151
Keasey, David Alan 143
Kimberley, Henry 21, 111

Lainton, Donald 128
Lawrence, Mr Justice 50
Lee, John 'Babbacombe' 14
Leech, Thomas Willoughby 89
Lewis, May 35
Lockley, Arthur 41
London, Reginald 104
Lush, Mr Justice 65
Lynskey, Mr Justice 110, 140
Lyons, Kitty 100

MacNaughton, Mr Justice 100
Maconochie, Capt. Alexander 9, 10, 11
Maksimowski, Piotr 113
Mansfield, Dr H.H. 90
Marney, Joan Mary 107
Matsell, Philip 23
McCann, Edmund 61
Medley, Det. Insp. Thomas 110
Merry, Harold Oswald 102
Millen, Det. Serg. Ernest 124
Mitchell-Innes, Mr Commissioner 77
Moore, Emma 39
Moran, Maggie 40
Mumford, Edith 43

Norton, Joe 62
Nugent, John 39

O'Connor, Bernard 59
O'Connor, Edward 58
O'Connor, Elizabeth 59
O'Connor, Ellen 59
O'Connor, Maggie 59